Praise for A Gift in Every Challenge

"I LOVED this book! The story Rose tells of her mother's life, and the impact it had on her own, will break your heart and have you smiling through your tears. You have not heard this one before.

Like many of us, Rose found the inspiration to change her life—and the mentoring that showed her HOW—between the pages of books written by people she had never met. With this book, she joins their esteemed ranks as she inspires and mentors you to take back your power and embark on your own journey to do it. Once you see what she and her mother faced and overcame, you will see your own challenges with new eyes. Your life will never be the same.

Rose will show you exactly how to have a different kind of conversation with yourself so you can choose to live an authentic life, no matter what circumstances you face. Don't wait another minute to buy this book!"

Maia Beatty
The Powerful Presence Trainer & Coach
Author of ***Dance into Your Power***

Praise for A Gift in Every Challenge

"Printed on a small wooden plaque in a gift shop was penned these words: "I am planning to have a nervous breakdown, I have earned it …I deserve it …I have worked hard for it …and nobody's going to keep me from having it."

It's easy to conclude "I just can't win!" and succumb to life's challenges. Rose underscores in this captivating read, "You CAN win!" Life's challenges when faced head-on and well can be building blocks – not barriers, leading to a meaningful and successful life.

Sandwiched between the sometimes shockingly transparent life experiences of her Mother and herself, Rose presents some sound life principles on how you can turn tragedy into triumph. J.B. Phillips paraphrased James 1:2-4 this way, "When all kinds of trials crowd into your lives, my brothers (and sisters), don't resent them as intruders, but welcome them as friends! Realize that they have come to test your endurance. But let the process go on until that endurance is fully developed, and you will find you have become men (and women) of mature character." Phillips provides here a pithy synopsis of this powerful read "A Gift in Every Challenge." I commend it to you."

Glen R. Pitts
The Barnabas Group

Praise for A Gift in Every Challenge

"A Gift in Every Challenge is an unforgettable book. You will be haunted by the pain and oppression endured by Mary and her children as well as being inspired by their courage, valor, and resourcefulness. In a time and a place where women were considered property at best, the remarkable women of the Lee family rose above poverty, sexism, racism, and abuse to build happy and secure lives.

Every woman who reads this book will be empowered and strengthened by its message."

Lynne Klippel
Author of Overcomers, Inc

"Dale Carnegie in his book *"How to Stop Worrying and Start Living"* said "If You Have a Lemon, Make a Lemonade". In my opinion, Rose Pellar is a lemonade connoisseur. I have known Rose for a little over six years and from her soft and gentle demeanor and spirit one would never imagine the story behind the smile. Because of her experience, Rose has a compassion to help people experiencing one of the most difficult challenges in life through her family law practice and divorce recovery workshops. In addition, her workshop, "The Gift of Love" which is aimed at helping couples strengthen their marriages, helped me and my wife to strengthen an already good marriage. I highly recommend *"A Gift In Every Challenge"* and believe it will be an encouragement to all who read it."

Paul Bailey
Lead Pastor, Lighthouse Community Church

A Gift in Every Challenge

Rose Pellar

BALBOA
PRESS

A DIVISION OF HAY HOUSE

Balboa Press books may be ordered through booksellers or by contacting:

Balboa Press
A Division of Hay House
1663 Liberty Drive
Bloomington, IN 47403
www.balboapress.com
1-(877) 407-4847

Because of the dynamic nature of the Internet, any web addresses or links contained in
this book may have changed since publication and may no longer be valid. The views
expressed in this work are solely those of the author and do not necessarily reflect the
views of the publisher, and the publisher hereby disclaims any responsibility for them.

The author of this book does not dispense medical advice or prescribe the use of any
technique as a form of treatment for physical, emotional, or medical problems without the
advice of a physician, either directly or indirectly. The intent of the author is only to offer
information of a general nature to help you in your quest for emotional and spiritual well-
being. In the event you use any of the information in this book for yourself, which is your
constitutional right, the author and the publisher assume no responsibility for your actions.

Any people depicted in stock imagery provided by Thinkstock are models,
and such images are being used for illustrative purposes only.
Certain stock imagery © Thinkstock.

Printed in the United States of America

ISBN: 978-1-4525-6630-6 (sc)
ISBN: 978-1-4525-6632-0 (hc)
ISBN: 978-1-4525-6631-3 (e)

Library of Congress Control Number: 2012924168

Balboa Press rev. date: 02/19/2013
First Printing: 2013

Dedication

THERE ARE INDIVIDUALS WHO ARE born before their time. In observing their thinking, their actions, and their courage, one cannot help but be in awe. Although I personally observed one such person and witnessed her accomplishments for almost four decades, I am still amazed and bewildered. It is with utmost gratitude and appreciation that I dedicate this book primarily to my mother, Mary Lee, otherwise known as Chin Lim Geow.

My mother was a very private person, and she often cautioned me not to air my dirty laundry because there would be individuals who would use the information against me or think less of me. Just as a doctor, however, prescribes an antibiotic because its benefits outweigh the possible side effects, I decided that the benefits to individuals who would be encouraged by my mother's story and my story would far outweigh any negative opinions that might be formed of me and my family.

My mother was a very modest woman. Even if she were alive today, she would not be able to admit that she was an inspiration to me and to my sister, let alone believe that the story of her life could be an inspiration to others who are fortunate enough to learn of it. She left me with a wonderful legacy, which I want to pass on to my children and grandchildren and my nephews and nieces and their children as well as the Lee offspring yet to be born.

My sons, Stephen and Christopher, have given me more credit than I believe I deserve for being a great mother. I am grateful for their regard and love for me. Since this book is also partially their story, it certainly is dedicated to them as well.

I include my grandchildren, who now provide me with another opportunity to pass on good moral values, a strong work ethic, and wisdom that I have acquired and am still acquiring. My goal is to cherish each moment I have with them, so that like my mom, when I am gone I will not be forgotten.

Violet, my dear sister, I owe you so much. You introduced me to the big world, did so much for me in my teen years and later became one of my biggest fans. We have shared so much and I honor you for being the magnet and the glue for the Lee family.

I also dedicate this book to my brothers, who were fellow sufferers with my sister and me during our childhood. Somehow we managed to bond together, finding joy in play and mischief amidst our troubled family life. My brother Donald was my constant companion in my teen years, and I remember fondly our countless trips to the record store, Sunday matinees, and teen birthday parties. As we were always with each other, we were often mistaken for young lovers. My brother Sterling was a trendsetter, the smooth talker, and the networker.

I dedicate this book especially to my late brother, Vincent, who was the most obvious victim of a dysfunctional family and whose untimely death in May 2010 was another tragedy in life he did not deserve. He is sorely missed.

I would be remiss if I did not also dedicate this book to Ted, my dear husband. I led a lifetime before God blessed me by bringing him into my life. His intelligence continually impresses me and his humor energizes me daily. I love that Ted demonstrate calmness toward me even though other things easily rattle him. I love our life and what he has added to it — his lovely children Erin and Matt and a fun-loving extended family. I anticipate with excitement the rest of our life together.

I dedicate this book also to all women who, despite having been victims of challenging circumstances, held on to hope, discovered their inner strength, found courage, and took action to overcome their challenges and become the wonderful persons they were meant to be.

Last, but certainly not least, I dedicate this book to you, the reader of my story. It is with you in mind that this book is written. Come with me on my journey of the life lessons I've learned. I share them with you not to impress you but to impress upon you that hardships, disappointments, and heartbreaks are merely challenges to help us grow into better, more resourceful, and, most importantly, happier people.

In life, problems are inevitable. How we deal
with them, however, is a choice.

One choice is to let your problems overwhelm you. The other
better choice is to view your problems as challenges.

The Oxford English Dictionary defines "problem" as
something difficult to deal with or understand"

On the other hand "challenge" is defined as
a call to try one's skill or strength.

Challenges are normally viewed as problems.

Choose instead to view every challenge as a gift

and

you will discover that there is indeed

a gift in every challenge.

Table of Contents

Foreword

IHAD THE OPPORTUNITY TO FIRST meet Rose Pellar in March 2011 when she attended my Writers' Retreat in St. George, Utah. Rose had already finished her manuscript and was in the process of editing her work. When I read the manuscript and spoke with Rose, I just knew her story had to be told.

The story of her mother's life demonstrates so vividly that with a firm belief in one's capability and taking action towards a worthy goal, one cannot help but succeed. Rose's story demonstrates the same conviction that you can succeed if you really believe and take action. Those two stories also demonstrate that challenges are opportunities for growth, and when both women decided not to succumb to a victim mentality, they each began to control their own destinies.

In this book, Rose has interspersed nuggets of wisdom and hope for the reader, and it is clear that Rose is not only a student of life but also a great teacher and role model for anyone who would like to lead a positive and rewarding life.

I have no doubt in my mind that this book will change lives. By changing one life, it will affect generations to come.

Leslie Householder
Best Selling Author of *The Jack Rabbit Factor*
Author of *Portal to Genius*
Co-Founder of School of Life Mastery

Preface

IT IS WITH SOME TREPIDATION that I write this book, because my personal life is now public. However, I share the stories with you in friendship and with trust.

Parts of this book will read like a novel. This allows you to draw from the stories the lessons *you* personally need. I share my story and my mother's story with you in the hope that you will deduce that challenges can be handled, no matter how insurmountable they seem. The steps are really simple: assess the situation, decide to change it, or not, believe you can, and take action. These steps can be summed up in these words: So What? Now What? Act!

In this book I also share with you words of wisdom that I have gathered over the years from my mentors—sage words that I paid thousands of dollars for in books, audio recordings, and courses. You may have heard or read these ideas before, but truth is always well worth repeating. You are reading this book because you were meant to read this book and I was meant to be your teacher. As presumptuous as that may seem, it has been said that "when the student is ready, the teacher will appear," and my experience has proved that to be so true. Whenever I needed to learn something, a book, an e-mail, or a recording would show up for the very lesson I needed to learn.

I say all this humbly because I am not by any means exactly where I want to be, but I am on a journey, just as you are. Sometimes the road is bumpy (bumpiness means we have lessons we need to learn) and we may not like the scenery (our interpretation of what is happening is what tells us whether the scenery is positive or negative). We will make progress, however, as long as we clearly focus on our goals, those goals are in line with who we are at our inner core, and we take each step of the journey confidently toward our destination. This book will help you along your journey,

Perhaps it may be that you are not now the person you want to be or you are not now where you want to be in your life. My sincere wish is that this book will spur you on to take the actions you need to change your circumstances.

I am very interested to have your feedback on how your thoughts about your challenges have been changed by this book and what you have decided to do *and* will do to overcome those challenges. As Grandmaster Tae Yun Kim (*The Silent Master—Awakening the Power Within*) says, "Everyone who comes into my life teaches me." So too, you are teachers to others. Share your successes with others and recommend this book to others you care about who may need to read it.

With humble gratitude,
Rose Pellar

Acknowledgments

I WOULD LIKE TO ACKNOWLEDGE ALL my family and friends who have supported me in my dream to write this book. Your encouragement sustained me throughout this process.

The many participants in the Divorce Recovery Workshops I co-facilitated over the past eight years who consistently told me "you should write a book" planted this idea into my head. The individuals who told me that my mother's story and my story inspired them to dare to dream and to take charge of their future, in turn, inspired me to share these stories in this form.

Countless individuals have touched my life and influenced me positively. Among them are the teachers in my mainstream education. However, I owe so much more to the many authors, speakers, and coaches in the areas of personal development, relationships, finances, real estate, and goal setting, whose works (books, seminars, courses, workshops, etc.) have helped to shape me over the past twenty years.

I acknowledge my publisher and its editors and staff for their wonderful assistance, support, encouragement, and advice. Without them I would have been like a ship lost at sea. Additionally, I acknowledge Leslie Householder for her insight and recommendations during our Writer's Retreat in March 2011. Her guidance cannot ever be repaid. The advice of Christine Klosser of Transformational Author Experience, and from Lynne Klippel of Business Building Books, was instrumental in shaping the finished product that you now have in your hands.

Lastly, I boldly thank God for sustaining me during my challenges and for all my blessings, especially those that came in the disguise of challenges.

Chapter 1

Life Requires Wise Choices and Authenticity

AS A FAMILY LAW ATTORNEY, I meet many individuals who drown in self-pity and who succumb too readily to a victim mentality as a result of a failed relationship. They are so consumed by the negativity of their situations that they fail to see that where there are problems, there are also opportunities.

We as individuals generally fail to take responsibility for our own lives. We tend to make excuses such as "If I hadn't had a bad childhood, I'd …"; "If my marriage hadn't ended, I'd …"; and "If I hadn't lost my job, I'd …" If, if, if … It's amazing how many of us give this little two-letter word, or someone else, so much power over our lives. Wouldn't you agree that it's time to take back our power and rid ourselves of the feeling of being helpless and stuck?

The fact is, whatever has happened is already in the past. Instead of saying, "If …" we need to have a different conversation with ourselves.

It is often difficult to set aside emotions connected with life changes and disappointments. Eventually, however, we do need to come to a place of emotional stability where we are able to acknowledge our emotions, understand them, master them, and make wise decisions in spite of them. I am neither a psychologist nor a psychiatrist, but my own experiences, as well as those of my countless clients, friends, and workshop participants, tell me this is what works best. I have learned that when we make choices for ourselves from a place that is congruent with who we truly are at our inner core (acting instead of reacting), and we choose to view our challenges not as burdens but as gifts to teach us very valuable lessons, we become empowered to lead an authentic and worthwhile life.

Some of us are able to recover quickly from bad situations; others cannot. We are all different. In the midst of challenges, it is important to remember that none of us is an island. We all need help or counseling in some form or another, whether it is from a doctor, a family therapist, a clergy member, a book, a coach, a mentor, or a trusted friend. Perhaps your trusted friend is your higher self or your Supreme Being. In my case, my trusted friend is God. Regardless of your source of wisdom, be careful to give that source only the amount of respect it truly deserves. You will see in a later chapter how I learned the hard way that not all counselors are worthy of that respect.

At the end of the day, no matter what conversations you have—nothing happens until you move your feet. Action is a necessary ingredient for change. Having a properly formulated and well-thought-out plan before you take action guarantees your results.

If this solution sounds very simplistic, it's because it is indeed very simple.

I could easily still be saying "if." When I reflect upon what I did to stop using *if* as a crutch, I have to say it was one book after another that showed up in my life to teach me a lesson I needed to learn at those particular times. In reading these books, I began to be inspired, and as a result I began to think differently. These books also led me to my mentors. As my thinking changed, I began to view situations differently, and when I took action with informed knowledge and purpose, not surprisingly my life began to transform.

I began my journey of growth when I first read about the experiences of others, and I learned from the insights they shared. Since everyone's story is unique, and each of us are teachers to others, I felt compelled to share my mother's story and my story to inspire others led by destiny to hold this book in their hands. I share with you my mother's story and my story in the hope that it will inspire you to make a decision to unwrap your current challenge and to take hold of its valuable gift. It could be a lesson you need to learn, or it could be that extra push you need to begin your journey to a new, incredible life.

We need to consciously and actively debunk the untold number of limiting beliefs, which society as a whole or individuals in positions of power (parents, teachers, ministers, and other well-meaning adults) have foisted upon us. This is essential if we are ever to succeed as happy, well-adjusted individuals. Let's not wait until we're drowning. Let's prepare ourselves and our children to swim countless laps in the pool of life.

This book relates the stories of two women—my mother and I—who refused to allow limiting cultural beliefs, gender bias, lack of education, financial constraints, violent or toxic relationships, a dysfunctional family, or societal or religious strictures to stop them from achieving their goals. The stories will inspire you to become resilient, to believe in your dreams, and to find the courage to pursue them.

This book is arranged into three portions. In the first group of chapters, I present the story of my mother's life. In the late 1930s, as a young woman, she journeyed from China across the world to Jamaica to join her husband. Amid personal abuse, economic hardship, and ethnic discrimination, she raised a family, ran small businesses, built houses, and won the respect of her community. I also reflect on the lessons she taught me.

In the next chapters, I describe my life growing up with my mother and father and my years as an adult. I was born in the Chinese immigrant community in Jamaica, and lived there into my adulthood, eventually raising children, settling in Ontario, Canada and remarrying . I describe the many ups and downs of my life and include observations about what I learned along the way.

The third portion of the book focuses on the life that you, the reader, are living. Taking the lessons I have learned from my mother's life and my own, along with wisdom from others whom I have studied, I provide practical encouragement about dealing determinedly with life's challenges and seeing the gift that each can provide. I previously have shared many of these insights with my legal clients, with a support group where I served as a facilitator, in speeches to women's groups, and in magazine articles. They are gathered here to inform and inspire you.

The lifesaving tools that are being handed to you in this book are simple techniques to help you deal with challenges. They encourage you to dream, to believe in your ability to succeed, and to take action.

There is indeed a silver lining behind every dark cloud. You need only push away that dark cloud and accept the gift that comes to you through challenges.

Chapter 2

One Strong Woman—My Mother's Story

The Journey Begins

On a slow boat from China, Chin Lim Geow started the day heaving into a bucket. Her stomach was empty, and she stopped just short of wishing she was dead. Seasickness was not the only cause of the sick feeling in the pit of her stomach. She was heading to a strange and faraway land—Jamaica in the West Indies—to start a new life. She had left her five-year-old daughter in the care of her mother-in-law in the Niu Fu village of Guangdong province. Lim Geow felt a heavy burden. "Mother-in-Law," as she called her, had borrowed heavily to pay Lim Geow's passage to join her husband, Lee Tse Tseung, in Jamaica. It would now be up to her to repay Mother-in-Law's debts.

It had been a couple of years since Lim Geow had been with her husband. He was unlike other men. He used to help her with chores and with their daughter. He was extra careful, however, not to be seen by others who would surely chastise him for being unmanly. Men and women each had their place in society at that time. Women were expected to work in the rice fields just as hard as the men, if not harder. Girls were regarded as useless, mainly because a girl eventually went to live with her husband's family and brought no value to her own family. Consequently, female babies were often drowned, abandoned by the roadside, or otherwise disposed of.

Lim Geow had thought herself very fortunate in the early days of her marriage because Tse Tseung had appeared to adore their little girl. *He's different from other men* she thought. She recalled how she had met her husband for the very first time on the day of her wedding and how frightened and embarrassed she had been when required to consummate the marriage while the wedding guests laughed knowingly outside their bedroom door. The firecrackers, which had been deliberately set off to conceal the deed, only served to unnerve her further.

Arranged marriages were the norm. Lim Geow had heard that the matchmaker had selected for her someone else who was reported to be a very good person. That match, however, was rejected by her own mother, who instead chose Tse Tseung as a match for her based on the criterion that Lim Geow should have a mother-in-law who would be kind to her. The fact that Tse Tseung had a bad reputation was ignored. Lim Geow's mother had a terrible mother-in-law, and so she was determined that Lim Geow would not suffer the same fate.

Tse Tseung's father ("Father-in-Law") lived in Jamaica. He had taken another wife in Jamaica several years earlier. She was not Chinese. She was a white woman who bore two other children for Father-in-Law. He was one of the many Chinese men who had more than one wife. Mother-in-Law, being the first wife, was considered to be the senior wife, referred to as "Tai Poh" (big wife), and the second wife was referred to as "Seh Poh" (little wife).

Father-in-Law had traveled to Jamaica as an indentured servant, and at the end of his term, he became an entrepreneur and a very successful businessman. Father-in-Law sought to have his son follow in his footsteps and so Tse Tseung had gone to Jamaica and his father had set him up as a shopkeeper. Reports reaching back to Mother-in-Law were that Tse Tseung was hopeless and Father-in-Law had given up on him. Mother-in-Law told Lim Geow that it was now up to her to go to Jamaica because she had to "rescue" Tse Tseung. Lim Geow did not know the extent of Tse Tseung's problems. Her sense of duty to Mother-in-Law and to her role of wife subdued her seasickness and sense of foreboding. Thoughts of how soon her own daughter would be able to join her and Tse Tseung in Jamaica sustained her during the long journey over rough seas.

During the journey she heard fellow passengers laughing at how the Chinese men in Jamaica were often "carrying coal." She voiced her consternation that the men should have such a menial job, but she was laughed at by the other passengers who enlightened her that the phrase "carrying coal" did not mean that the men were physically carrying coal. It was a term used to indicate that the Chinese men were sleeping with the black women.

The ship eventually docked in Kingston, Jamaica. In the crowd she recognized a few people she knew who had preceded her from her home town but Tse Tseung was nowhere to be seen.

Disappointment after Disappointment

Fortunately, friends took Lim Geow in. Inquiries showed that Tse Tseung was living in Cross Keys in the Parish of Manchester some miles from Kingston. She imagined that something was terribly wrong with her husband. Why else was he not there to meet her? Lim Geow, traveling by horse and buggy, eventually arrived at the place where Tse Tseung ran a grocery store. Instead of being happy to see her, however, he was angry, demanding to know why she had come.

She choked on her disappointment. The purpose of her journey to this strange, foreign land seemed all for naught. She was only twenty years old. She had left her young child to join a rogue on a one-way ticket. She had no means of returning to China, even if she would want to do so. She had discovered that Tse Tseung was on the verge of bankruptcy because he was a heavy gambler. There were other surprising facts about her husband she would soon learn.

Her night of reunion with Tse Tseung was not spent in the same bed with him. His Jamaican lover had that privilege. Lim Geow instead reclined on a pile of wooden crates, shifting painfully. She was forced to spend the next several nights on those crates and tried to make the best of it.

Her thoughts would not quiet themselves as she tried to determine what choices she had. Everything seemed hopeless, yet she could not bring herself to cry. Her insides felt as if they had been ripped out and her heart felt as if it would explode.

Her arrival supplied Tse Tseung's creditors with a presumably valid reason why he had been unable to pay his debts. After all, his creditors reasoned, did he not have to spend money to bring his wife over from China? It brought him a reprieve and further extensions of credit.

This would not be the last time that she was his redeemer.

Stiff Upper Lip

Lim Geow assessed the situation. She saw no alternative. She somehow had to earn enough money to provide for her, send for her daughter, and repay Mother-in-Law's debt.

Speaking no English and with no immediate family to help her, she decided to keep a stiff upper lip. She watched and learned how to sell goods in the shop, learning the money system (pounds, shillings, and pence), as she made little notes in her exercise notebook in her poor Chinese writing. Like all girls in China, she had not attended school. It was considered a waste of time and resources. In fact, even rice was considered "thrown away" if it was fed to girls. With that cultural backdrop, it was no wonder she felt she had to take what life handed her.

She began to draw upon her inner strength. Later in life she identified this inner strength as her unfailing reliance on a merciful and loving God.

She settled with her lot in life, even to care for Tse Tseung's two illegitimate children by his paramour. In China it was not uncommon for wives to live together and take care of each other's children. Asked later in life why she even gave the time of day to Tse Tseung's illegitimate children, Lim Geow's goodness showed in her answer. "The children are innocent. It is not their fault," she said.

The grocery business began to do well, and it is questionable whether Tse Tseung realized that the success was due to Lim Geow's hard work and her respectful nature with the customers. If he did, he never showed it. She felt it was her duty to be a good wife, and a part of her wanted to believe that by her being a good wife, he would mend his ways. Her expectations were short lived. The draw of the mah-jongg tables proved overpowering, and Tse Tseung spent his nights and days gambling away whatever profits the store brought in.

Eventually, his paramour moved out, because together he and she were like dynamite and a lit match. Lim Geow learned that his paramour had taken an axe to him and left a scar on his brow as a reminder.

At some point, Tse Tseung convinced Lim Geow to have relations with him. A miscarriage broke her heart. She had been on her feet from 5:00 a.m. until 8:00 p.m. each day, hardly finding time to eat. Her daily practice was to work at the store, care for her family, and then stay up late at night to sew her underwear and clothing. They were made from bags in which chicken feed, cornmeal, and flour were delivered to the store. The chicken feed bags were flower patterned and colored, whereas the flour and cornmeal bags were of a coarse beige material. With the miracle of colored Jiffy dyes, the clothing made from the flour and cornmeal bags were transformed into fetching dresses sewn by hand.

Shortly after the miscarriage, Lim Geow again conceived, and this time she bore him a son, Sterling. Tse Tseung's manly pride about again being a father wore off before too long. He continued to womanize and gamble. When his financial situation had improved, he kicked Lim Geow out of the home and shop. She left with a small bundle of clothes and with their young son in tow. Tse Tseung vowed that wherever she ended up, his shadow would never cross her doorstep, even if he became bankrupt.

An Entrepreneur Is Born

With the help of friends, Lim Geow found a shop, which she rented. She had established a good business relationship with one of the main suppliers of grocery items in Kingston and was able to take goods on consignment.

Not only was it unheard of that a woman in the early 1940s would own a grocery business, but also it was downright scandalous that a Chinese woman, a single mother to boot, could do so.

The customers liked and respected "Madam" or "Miss Chin," as they called her. It was a common practice for Jamaicans to call all Chinese individuals Mr. Chin or Miss Chin. Madam always smiled, and the twinkle in her eyes belied any hardships she had been encountering. Life was not exactly how she had pictured it would be, but she was grateful. She was not homeless, she had her health, and she had food to eat and a means to earn a living. She began to make headway and for that she gave thanks daily.

She balanced her young child on her hip as she handed the groceries over the counter to the customer, collected the money, and made change. When goods were delivered she marked an "X" to indicate she had received them. By the grace of God, no one attempted to cheat her.

She learned some words, especially those related to groceries. She made Chinese characters in her little exercise book to match the phonetic English words. She had connected with some relatives who also ran grocery stores. Her store was compact, roughly twelve by eighteen feet in area. When she could, she traded stories with the other grocery store owners, finding out what prices were being charged for food and other items, what was selling, and how to improve her inventory.

She dealt honestly and fairly with everyone, whether they were suppliers, the delivery person or the customers. She listened to the customers' requests and if she had enough requests for certain goods and products, she stocked them. She heard of other shopkeepers who sneakily put a thumb down on the scales to increase the weight of the flour, cornmeal, or sugar in order to cheat the customers, and she steadfastly refused to do that. She felt it was dishonest, and she valued her customers. There was no doubt that a guilty conscience was not the reason she lay awake at night. What kept her awake was the question of how she could protect her children and provide for them.

The Shadow Crossed Her Doorstep

Financially, she was making progress and then … the shadow of Tse Tseung crossed her doorstep. He was penniless, and his paramours had deserted him, as he was unable to support them. Reluctantly, Lim Geow accepted him back into her life. She knew in her heart of hearts this was not going to be a bed of roses, except for the thorns.

It was just easier to conform to what the Chinese community and her culture expected of her and that was to be with her husband. The only problem was that it required her to be the breadwinner; the mother and the father; and the wife, controlled and abused by her husband. (Sadly, more than sixty-six years later, too many women still settle for less than what they deserve.)

Accepting her lot in life, she continued to work in the shop morning to night, as well as cooking and cleaning and taking care of her children. She bore another son, Vincent.

Before Vincent there was another child, Lucky. He was called Lucky because he appeared to change Tse Tseung's luck for the better whenever Lucky came alongside him at the mah-jongg table. Lucky, however, was not as fortunate as his name suggested. One late night while sharing the bed with Lim Geow and Tse Tseung, Lucky's pee trickled down his legs onto Tse Tseung's head. The poor two-year-old toddler did not know what caused him to sail through the air and to land on the hard wooden floor. Lim Geow collected Lucky and hushed him until he fell asleep.

The next morning Lucky was dead. Lim Geow wondered if she could survive another tragic personal loss, because it felt as if once more her heart was about to explode right into her brain.

Convinced by relatives that reporting the incident to the authorities would result in both Tse Tseung and her being imprisoned, thus leaving Sterling and Vincent abandoned, she decided not to report that her son Lucky was the fatal victim of Tse Tseung's violent temper. In her mind, she reasoned that she could not bring Lucky back and she had to care for Sterling and Vincent. That was now her duty.

Tse Tseung turned insolent once more and kicked her out of the shop and home. This time she had two children, Sterling and Vincent, in tow. She was despondent, and the burden seemed heavier. She vowed, however, to do whatever she could to ensure that her children received the necessities of life and care until they could care for themselves.

Her network of relatives and friends rescued her, giving her short-term shelter and food until she found another home and shop. Her word and good character were her only references. There was no social assistance, and she did not go looking for another man to take care of her. She simply relied on her inner strength and her unwavering belief in God.

She did open another shop, and in a short span of time she started to make a small profit, but it seemed she was working morning until night, day after day. She was exhausted.

In almost no time at all, Tse Tseung, having again run his own shop into the ground, and fleeing from his gambling debts, turned up again at her doorstep. He manipulated and used to his advantage Lim Geow's sense of duty to convince her to take him in. Tse Tseung behaved for a while, giving her a false sense of hope. Furthermore, she believed, as did the Chinese community, that it was extremely important to avoid embarrassment and shame. So far, she had not been able to avoid them. She was under the control of Tse Tseung and he had already brought shame upon her by throwing her out more than once like a used dirty dishrag. He also brought her woes.

Tse Tseung was not a kind man by nature, and although he managed to charm the Jamaican women he slept with, his manners to the shop's customers stung like the quills of a porcupine. He habitually cursed out customers, and on one occasion he crossed the wrong person. She was what Jamaicans call an "*obeah* woman." This woman vowed to cast a spell on him in retaliation. Tse Tseung went unscathed. Lim Geow, however, became extremely ill, and the doctor could not determine the nature of the ailment. Ngee Geow Jah, a close relative, became concerned and decided that Lim Geow's illness could only have been caused by *obeah*, or witchcraft. After consultation with another lady who engaged in this dark art, Lim Geow was told she was hexed and that only a high-ranking practitioner could remove the spell. All it took to be cured was for Lim Geow to pay ten pounds, a tidy sum of money then, and to drink a brew prepared for her. She did this, and she got better.

Noticing later that Lim Geow had recovered, the *obeah* woman said she cast a spell on Lim Geow. The woman indicated she tried to put a hex on Tse Tseung, but the candle she lit for him did not flicker, indicating that he was untouchable. Consequently, the woman decided to cast a spell on Lim Geow to indirectly hurt Tse Tseung. Little did the *obeah* woman know that he could have cared less about Lim Geow's health, except for the fact that she was his meal ticket.

Saved by Good Character

There was an uprising against the Chinese in a rural part of Jamaica outside Kingston. The Chinese were perceived to be a threat because it appeared they were prospering—owning shops and making money. Wielding machetes and moving in throngs, many local residents terrorized the Chinese shopkeepers, injuring and killing some. Upon arrival at Lim Geow's shop, the throng was angry and cursing. Out of nowhere four black men jumped up onto the counter and shouted to the angry mob, "Do not harm this woman. She is a good woman. Kill the Chinaman if you want, but do not touch this woman." Her kindness and respect for everyone saved Tse Tseung's hide. He should have been eternally grateful, but he was not. His carousing and gambling and abuse continued.

Even with the hardships that Lim Geow continued to endure, she managed to keep sending money to Mother-in-Law for the child she had left behind in China and for Mother-in-Law's debt. The ache and emptiness for her child never dimmed. She kept hoping and praying that one day she would be reunited with her. This was just one of the many goals she had made for herself. She also needed to repay Mother-in-Law and to care for her other children, who, upon the arrival of Violet in 1944, numbered three after another miscarriage.

"A girl, not a girl!" Tse Tseung swore. "Who needs a girl child? They're a waste of time, money, and rice." Violet was lucky she wasn't born in China, for who knows what her fate may have been. There were moments of normalcy in the family, but the cursing and swearing at everyone, especially Violet and Lim Geow, continued. His roster of swears to Lim Geow included "I'll rape your mother." This portrayed the man's disrespect of women in general, and his swears and threats sounded too real to be dismissed lightly. He threatened to kill her and the children. When he did not get enough money to gamble, he terrorized the family until Lim Geow caved in. Oftentimes, he grabbed whatever clothing, shoes, and plants he could get his hands on and burned them to intimidate her. She knew she needed to protect the children, no matter what, even if it meant staying with a tyrant. She wasn't so concerned for her own safety.

Handing the Children to God's Care

Dreams often guided her. In one such vivid dream, she found herself in a meadow that was parched and dry. She looked up at the hill, where she saw a lady with beautiful blue eyes and a long robe. Where this lady stood the grass was green and lush beneath her feet, whereas all around the land was parched and dry.

The lady beckoned Lim Geow to approach her. As Lim Geow started to do so, she noticed that Tse Tseung was following her. Sensing this lady to be special, she beseeched her not to have Tse Tseung follow her, because he was a bad person. The lady said, "I know, but you must bear your burden. He is your burden."

As she reached the lady, the lady said, "My name is Mary and your name is Mary too." Lim Geow was swept over by a feeling of peace.

Two weeks after this dream, she accepted an invitation from a lady to go with her to church. As she walked into the huge Roman Catholic cathedral on North Street, she noticed a statue. She was taken aback by the resemblance to the lady in her dream and even more amazed when she learned it was a depiction of Mary, the mother of Jesus.

After attending church for some time, Lim Geow decided to become baptized in the Roman Catholic faith, and for her Christian name she took on the name of Mary. She was now Mary Lee. Although she did not quite understand the rituals or the sermons or the language used, she sensed that this place brought her closer to God. She commenced praying to God for help throughout the day and at night. She said, "God, I do not know how to raise these children. I leave them in your hands to take care of them." She also learned to call on God's help when in distress and she asked God to send angels to assist her. She shared throughout the years many stories of how after praying for God's help someone would show up to help her. Her trust in God grew stronger over the years.

On Sunday mornings she awakened the children quietly and got them dressed for church. By 5:00 a.m. she and the children were out the door to walk approximately thirty minutes for the 6:00 a.m. Mass that got her back home before Tse Tseung was awake. As long as he was not inconvenienced and he did not see that she was being devoted to something or someone other than him, she was safe.

The early services also got her back in time for her to get the shop ready for opening. This entailed cleaning out the glass bread case with a vinegar and water solution. Warm, fresh bread was delivered each day to the shop and particularly on Sundays the sale of hard dough bread and butter was brisk.

In many ways, Lim Geow also handed her own life over to God's care. It would have been easy for her to stay in bed to get some extra sleep, but it was important to her to attend Mass and give thanks for her blessings. Others may have questioned what she had to be thankful for, but as long as she had life and opportunities she considered herself extremely blessed and she kept her faith that the Almighty "Massa God," as she referred to Him, would guide and protect her and her children. In so many ways He did.

God's Displeasure

Tse Tseung knew only few things: how to gamble, how to womanize, and how to make babies. Lim Geow had a boy child, Donald, in 1946. He was a tiny one, the size of a small glass bottle, but Donald grew well.

L-R: Sterling, Donald, Papa, Vincent, Mama and Violet

Friends and relatives berated her for having so many children. She had no idea about contraceptives and she did not have the courage to refuse Tse Tseung. Once more she conceived. Under pressure, she had an abortion. It was a girl. The abortion almost killed her, and in her weakened state she grew hot with fever and writhed in agony. Finally she succumbed to sleep. Her dream this time was very disturbing. She again saw Mary, the mother of Jesus, but Mary ignored her, and when Lim Geow attempted to approach her, Mary denounced her for having had the abortion. Lim Geow awakened with resolution that she did not want to be distanced from God, who surely must be displeased with her, so the next time she became pregnant, she did not give in to the urgings of her well-meaning relatives and friends to have another abortion.

A Rose by Any Other Name

On a cool December day, I entered the world unaware of what was before me. This was when I joined my mother, Lim Geow (Mama), and my siblings on their journey through life. And, oh yes, Tse Tseung (Papa) also.

Behind the locked door, Mama writhed and moaned in agony as the midwife sternly shouted out instructions to her. My siblings (Sterling, Vincent, Violet, and Donald) were outside the locked door, crying. They were confused. Why was Mama moaning in pain? Was it possible that Mama was being hurt by the tall, heavy black woman inside, who always smelled of mint when she burped loudly? Papa swore at the children to shut up. Mama could not wait to be done with the childbirth so that she could get to her other children to calm the situation in order not to anger Papa any further.

Rose was the name the midwife gave to me. She must have been obsessed with flowers, since she named my older sister Violet.

Papa's reaction to another girl was predictable. *Hyak lung mee* (a waste of rice), he muttered.

L-R: Donald, Sterling, Vincent, Violet (Me in the center)

Hard Choices

Life continued to have its ups and downs, mostly downs for Lim Geow, otherwise known as Mary Lee, my Mama.

In about 1953, Mama gave up the business at Victoria Street, and she and the entire family moved to a location at Luke Lane in downtown Kingston. It was a rental accommodation above a warehouse. It was strange living in an upstairs apartment in a commercial part of Kingston. The apartment was situated next door to a bar, and most evenings music could be heard blaring from the jukebox.

On the other side of the building was a bottling plant.

Just a few doors up on the opposite side of the road was an ice cream parlor, above which Mama's friend, Sam Geow, lived. Sam Geow was a more modern Chinese woman who delighted in referring to me as "white gal." Apparently, my skin was very fair and my hair was reddish brown. Most people who did not know I was Mama's daughter thought that I was her grandchild because of my hair coloring and complexion and because Mama had me later in life.

The explanation for my coloring and complexion, I heard years later, was that it was traceable to the wife of Mama's grandfather, who had gone to the United States as a farmhand and ended up marrying the American farmer's daughter.

From the apartment, there was a bird's eye view of the street. One evening Violet spotted Papa from the window walking down the street holding hands with his girlfriend. Violet shouted out "Peel Head John Crow" (this translates to "Bald Headed Vulture"). This was Violet's name for Papa's girlfriend. Minutes later Papa ran up the stairs and immediately went for Violet, only to be blocked by Mama.

Mama had apparently been scouting around for another shop, and within a few months she was able to acquire a business at Gold Street, also in Kingston.

This was a much larger store. She did very well, managing to satisfy Papa's demands for gambling money as well as taking care of the children's needs.

The shop was across from a dance hall, which had dances on Friday and Saturday nights. These dances often ended up in brawls, and on one or two occasions patrons were stabbed or killed. On the other corner was a brothel. Very soon after the ships came into port, we observed the sailors entering the brothel. Sometimes, fifteen or so minutes later, the sailors came scurrying out in partial states of undress followed hot on their heels by a military policeman brandishing a billie stick. On the third corner was a bar. Brawls outside of the bar were common, and more often than not a brawl involved two prostitutes physically fighting over a sailor.

Despite the environment, or maybe because of it, business was booming. Mama had the foresight to add an ice cream parlor to the shop, from which she sold many types of ice cream and cold Red Stripe beer. There was a bustling business to be done on weekends when naval ships were in the harbor. The sailors brought in and treated the prostitutes to ice cream cones, and the sailors downed a couple of beers. The sailors inevitably left a dollar coin as a tip. At first Mama would push back the money toward the sailors, thinking they had overpaid her. She quickly learned that this was money she could keep. It was therefore a hard decision for her to give up the business after a neighboring friend, Chin Sui Pin, a justice of the peace, told Mama, "This is not the environment in which to raise children, particularly girls. You need to protect them and keep them away from this kind of environment."

She was reluctant to give up the lucrative business but she chose the higher good—what was in the best interests of her children. She thought that she now had enough money to buy a piece of property and build a house for her family. She hired a contractor who did all the preliminary work, including buying the materials, hiring the workers, and building the house. It was quite exciting to move into a house as opposed to living behind a store or above a warehouse.

Within a few months of moving in, Mama realized there was no money coming in, and whatever money she had made from the sale of the business and had managed to save was quickly dwindling. She put her thoughts to finding a way to earn an income. She had to, because she had five children with her who ranged from seven years old to seventeen, another child in China, and a husband who contributed nothing to the family financially or otherwise. He was simply a drain.

Mary Lee, the Builder

She thought it a good idea to buy another piece of land, build on it, and sell that house in order to make money. She bought the property just down the road and hired the same contractor, and construction began. This time, however, was different. She was on the job site each day to keep a watchful eye on how things were being done and to learn what was required to build a house.

The finished home was on a huge piece of land and was quite impressive with at least four bedrooms, two bathrooms, spacious dining and living rooms, and terrazzo tiles. Upon completion of the house, she tried to sell it, but no one put in an offer. Instead a buyer wanted the house we lived in. She decided "money is money" and she sold the house we lived in to move down the road to the newly built house. The sale proceeds allowed her to take care of the family's needs for a while.

The money dwindled once more, and Mama reckoned, *I can do the same thing again in order to earn more money.* She looked around in the neighborhood, found a lot that was ten to fifteen minutes away by bus, and bought it. This time she drew up her own rough plans on a piece of paper, inserted the room sizes on the plan, and figured out the square footage. She had a draftsperson make up the blueprint, to be approved by the City. Next she bought the materials and hired the workers, and construction began. Hence, she became Mary Lee, the builder.

Each morning she took the bus and went to the job site. At the site, she sat on her bench with a wide-rim straw hat, observing and learning.

The construction began with the digging of the foundation. A ritual, maybe Jamaican or Chinese, required a rooster to be killed and its blood sprinkled in the newly dug foundation to ward off evil spirits. A Chinese ritual also required that dishes of food be placed in the corner of the rooms prior to moving in, to appease the spirits. Although

Mama believed unwaveringly in God, she held on to the superstitions of both the Chinese and Jamaican culture along with the Catholic faith. She chose to play it safe. A priest came to bless the house when it was completed. The parish priest, Father Glavin, attended, said prayers, and sprinkled holy water in all the rooms. After the blessing, he sat and enjoyed a piece of cake and a glass of port.

The house structure was concrete block and steel. Once the foundation was dug, a steel worker wired together the steel foundation and uprights. The blocks were then put onto and in between the steel uprights. Cement was poured inside and between the blocks to hold them together. Just from observing that first house being built, Mama was able to instruct a young worker on how to mix mortar. She communicated in broken English. She gently pushed aside the young lad and told him "no" to indicate he was doing it wrong. She then took the shovel and turned the cement, gravel, sand, and water mixture to show him how it was done.

Each Friday, which was payday, she knew exactly what to pay to each worker. Her trip to the bank for the payout resulted in her bringing back for each worker the exact amount of cash due. In her exercise book she wrote her Chinese character for each worker, whether it was a carpenter, a plumber, a steel person, or a painter. Beside each worker's identifying mark, she wrote in the amount he was to be paid, and the person was required to sign his name, or mark his "X" if he was illiterate, to signify having received his pay.

The workers all respected her. They did not take advantage of her, and they spoke to her in a respectful manner, because she always respected them. When the house was completed and she tried to sell, there was no buyer. Instead, an offer was received for the house we lived in. This meant we had to move once more. This scenario repeated itself several times over and the family was constantly living in new houses. Outsiders could not have guessed that financially Mama was struggling.

When I was ten or eleven, old enough to be able to calculate the square footages for Mama, she pushed toward me the paper on which she'd drawn boxes for the bathrooms and other rooms with the

21

dimensions inside the boxes. Mama said to me, "Work out the square footage." I wasn't sure of what I was doing or whether it was right. There were no calculators back then, or if there were, I had none available to me. Often on the first go-around, when I provided her with my result, she would look at me, shake her head and say, "No, do it again." She had made her own mental calculations, and my numbers did not match. When I did the calculation again, she sometimes said, "It's too large," and she then made adjustments to the dimensions. This process was repeated until Mama was satisfied that she had the right square footage to fit her budget.

Her next step was to take the plans to a draftsperson responsible for making up the blueprint to show the width of the walls and the placement of windows, doors, and all the electrical wiring and plumbing fixtures, etc. Following the plans being completed, she took them to the City for approval. Once the plans were approved, she ordered the materials, and lined up the workers.

This was a woman with no education, who could not read, write or speak English. My sister Violet once remarked that if Mama had been educated, she would have been dangerous! Mama supported her five kids living with her as well as her oldest child who was being cared for by Mother-in-Law in China. In addition, she was repaying Mother-in-Law's debt and also supporting Tse Tseung. She accepted these responsibilities dutifully. At a closer look, this was not all she did. She had set herself a goal—to protect and support her children until they were able to support themselves and to bring them up as responsible citizens. She kept that goal firmly fixed in her mind and her heart believed it was possible. She didn't just engage in wishful thinking, she did everything she could to achieve her goal. In doing so, she succeeded in accomplishing her goal. Had I not witnessed it myself, I would not have believed it.

A Trailblazer

Mama not only did what others said would be impossible for her to do but she also became an example for others. A younger relative of hers, Noel Lee Fatt, had the wisdom to seek her advice. He thought that if an uneducated woman who could not speak, read, or write English could build houses and make money, certainly so could he. He was male, he was educated, and he could read, write, and speak English. Furthermore, he had some money to fund his start. Mama was an unselfish woman, and she shared her knowledge and experience with him. She was in essence his mentor. Noel went on to build many houses and he did it well. He turned a very sizeable profit for himself and for his family. At Mama's funeral he told me that he owed his success to her.

Another Chinese gentleman, Thomas Lue Fook, also decided to follow Mama's lead, building houses but to a lesser degree.

Ruled by a Tyrant

Mama celebrated Christmas in a small way. We did not have a Christmas tree. That was not our custom. We did have a special dinner, but it was not turkey and ham. Dinner consisted of special Chinese dishes, such as chicken and black mushrooms (*Dung Goo Guy*), pork and wood fungus (*Muk Nyee Ju Nyuk*), fish maw and chicken soup (*Um Peow Sun*), and my favorite: pork and yams (*Keyw Nyuk*). We would also have stir-fried Chinese vegetables with squid cut up in such a way it curled up into tiny tubes when fully cooked, and of course boiled white rice. We knew these were considered delicacies and that it was a treat.

Mama also made sure my sister Vi and I got new dresses for Christmas. We wore our dresses for weddings and all other special occasions the following year. They were sewn a little bigger than normal so we could grow into them.

Amidst the turmoil, Mama managed to make us feel special. For instance, whenever one of us had a birthday, the birthday child was given a hard-boiled egg for breakfast. The egg was symbolic of birth and it was special. We didn't get huge birthday presents. As matter of fact, I can't recall ever getting a birthday present when we were younger. We instinctively knew that it wasn't something that was done and we accepted it. We did not feel deprived although others may think we were truly deprived because of the lack of birthday presents. We were just happy to have a roof over our heads, a bed to sleep in, food to eat, and clothes on our bodies. It may not have been much, but we had the necessities of life, and Mama reminded us to be thankful for our blessings.

As kids, Sterling, Vincent, Violet, and Donald played together often. One Christmas they decided to have a Christmas tree. Improvising, they broke a branch from a tree and used foil from cigarette packages to trim the tree. Papa was enraged and he kicked down the makeshift tree and broke off a piece to use as a switch. The children all ran away except for Sterling. Vincent ran off to hide under the cellar ... Tse Tseung threw stones into the cellar at him and eventually poured boiling water down through the floor boards in an attempt to flush him out. Incensed that Vincent and Violet and Donald had managed to escape, Tse Tseung decided to take his frustrations out on Sterling, who had not run away and who had apologized. He beat Sterling with the switch.

Fortunately, the children were not deterred by this tyrant and often found things to amuse themselves, sometimes at the risk of getting a beating from Tse Tseung. He hated Violet from the day she was born and he looked for any opportunity to shove her or punch her in the chest. We children referred to him as "Papa," but there was no real connection to what that title meant. He was not a parent in any sense of the word. He was not the financial provider. He was not the caregiver and certainly, he was not a role model. Anything that defined what a father is, he was not. He boasted to outsiders about his business, when all he ever did was to find opportunities to siphon money from the shop to fund his bad habits. When there was no longer a shop, he even went as far as to take toothpastes and other household items from our home to give to his paramours. Yet there were many who actually believed he was the provider of the family. He talked a good talk.

He disappeared for periods of time when the gambling was good and when his paramours found time for him. When he was away, we children felt a relief similar to when you stop banging your head against the wall. Typically, when Tse Tseung returned he was bad tempered—ranting, raving, swearing, and pushing his weight around. It was like a dark cloud had descended upon the family, who paid the price for Papa's losses at the mah-jongg table. We children often wondered to ourselves why Mama suffered his moods and his treatment, but we never spoke up about it to Mama or Papa.

As all children are apt to do, as we got older we pushed the envelope a bit. On a few occasions, Vincent took Papa's bicycle for a ride without asking and somehow balanced Violet, Donald, and Sterling on the bicycle. Sometimes they were caught, and Papa unleashed his wrath once more. Mama was a peacemaker and reminded the children to be respectful. Tse Tseung, after all, was their father.

Mama had to struggle to convince him that the children needed an education even though he was not the one paying for it. She knew if he did not approve, there would be hell to pay. Sterling, the oldest of the five of us, commenced schooling at the age of eleven. Luckily, he was intellectually bright and caught on very quickly, graduating from high school—Kingston College—with flying colors. Vincent, on the other hand, had very little schooling before conflicts with Papa required that he leave home and school at the tender age of fourteen.

Violet's anger and hate for Papa consumed her, and after being shoved around once too often, she stood her ground, faced off with him, and told him in no uncertain terms that if he ever touched her again, one of them would be taken away in a coffin and it was not going to be her! Thereafter, Papa stopped punching Violet in her chest as he had been doing on a regular basis. He must have seen in her eyes that she meant it. It did not stop him from swearing at her, and there were occasional arguments between them, but he knew not to go any further.

Papa then commenced to pick on Donald, nagging at him, cutting up the football Donald had been playing with, and generally threatening him. Papa feigned an interest in Donald's school work, but it was just an excuse to nag and prevent him from having any fun. Donald, like Violet, was pushed too far. It was the summer of 1959 when Donald lost it. He grabbed a cleaver, put it in front of him on the dining table, and dared Papa to hit him with the belt that he held in his hand. From then on, Papa stopped his threats and never attempted again to beat any of the children.

The interesting phenomenon was that none of the children showed any disrespect to Papa, even after the showdowns. Nevertheless, he continued to presume himself to be worthy of respect and in different ways made the children's lives unbearable and miserable. He complained to Mama about the children's behavior, telling her she had to do something about it. None of the children misbehaved, but the tyrant had to rule. He curtailed the length of time the children spent in the shower. He complained that the children were wasting water as well as the propane used to heat the water. Even though the children knew he had not earned any of the money to pay for the water or propane, they tried to listen when he complained. It was difficult to do so after a day at the beach when the sand was buried in hair, ears, and everywhere. The children knew he would continue to gripe and complain to Mama, and so for her sake they tried not to make life difficult for her. Papa complained also about the children wasting electricity, and if we had not finished our homework by 8:00 p.m.—too bad, the lights went out. Oftentimes, the children used a flashlight under the covers to finish cramming for exams. It seemed a miracle that any of us children graduated from high school.

In contrast, Mama disciplined by lecturing and by telling mythical stories. One such story was of a child who did not respect her mother and found she could not escape the lightning until she apologized and began to respect her mother. Another story she told to teach humility was of a little girl whose mother had brought home apples from the market. The apples varied in sizes and when the girl selected an apple, she picked the smallest one. When the mother questioned her selection, the girl replied, "Since I'm the smallest one in the family I chose the smallest apple." Mama often taught the children valuable lessons using parables. A look from Mama was all it took for the children to know they were doing something wrong and to immediately stop. She taught us to be respectful to adults and to always be polite. When offered anything by others, we children always looked her way to get her approval before accepting. She was in charge of us children and we knew it. The irony was that the tyrant was in charge of her.

We were no doubt scarred from a dysfunctional childhood, but we learned from Mama to interpret what happened to us in a positive light.

Protecting the Innocent

Papa did not support, nor did he contribute in any way toward, the family whose lives he made very difficult. There were constant arguments. He threw temper tantrums and threatened lives constantly. Vincent was unwilling to suffer Papa's unreasonable behavior toward Mama or any of his other siblings, let alone himself. As a result, Vincent and Papa butted heads constantly. It became physical. Papa threatened with axes, pick axes, and shovels, and Vincent was his constant target. Sending Vincent to Alley, a small town northwest of Kingston, was Mama's solution to protect the fourteen-year-old Vincent. She saw that no good could come out of the ongoing battles between Papa and Vincent. She seemed to know the extent to which Papa would go to win the battle, and she was not prepared to lose another child.

Vincent came home for short periods of time, whereupon Papa resumed his attacks on him. Fortunately, Vincent eventually decided to go seek adventure in England in the late 1950s. He did stunt work in the movie industry and was on location in Spain before he returned to London. Shortly after his return to England, he was introduced to Marisa, a Spanish girl from Madrid who came to England to be an *au pair* girl in order to learn English. They married soon after meeting and had a child, Ricky.

When Vincent had been a youngster, Mama had been able to protect him from physical harm. Many years later, however, at nearly the age of seventy, Vincent died a horrible death. It was in 2010. While Vincent was working to repair a sign above ground level, the cherry picker he was riding in contacted high-voltage wires and he was electrocuted. There were burns on more than 60 percent of his body. Who knows whether Vincent could have avoided this terrible fate? In trying to make sense of this tragedy, one might wonder whether he would have been able to have a different career and to retire earlier if he had not had to find safe haven from Tse Tseung and had he been afforded the opportunity of an education. Without meaning to absolve Tse Tseung of culpability of the harm he caused to those whose care he was entrusted with, or to cause any affront to Vincent's family, let me say that my belief is that regardless of what life throws at us, ultimately we make decisions for ourselves in light of circumstances and we are responsible for those decisions. Having said that, I just wish Vincent's life was easier, and I miss him so much.

Resourcefulness

Mama also found others ways to supplement her income. She did not rely solely on building houses; she also took in tenants. We were fortunate enough to have a gentleman named Mr. Chong and his son, Dalton, rent a room in our house. We had no idea what Mr. Chong did for a living, but he went off each morning as if to work. His wife had taken their daughter with her and left him with his son. As a boarder, his son ate meals with us. Mr. Chong became like a surrogate father because he brought us candies, sat with us, and told us stories. Many were ghost stories that left me too terrified to go to sleep. He took Violet, Donald, and me to Coney Island a few times, and he became the father that we never had. Papa made allegations that Mama was having an affair with Mr. Chong but we knew it was not true. Not only was there absolutely no opportunity, there was no way Mama would have done such a thing. She was a woman of integrity and always did what was right. She did, however, talk with him, and she enjoyed his company.

Mama caved in to the urgings of Papa and she asked Mr. Chong and his son to find alternative lodgings. She missed the extra income as well as the companionship of Mr. Chong. I missed him also.

At our next house, Mama rented rooms to another couple, the Fongs, who had a young son, Milton, and a daughter, Jennifer. This was only for a short time as well, since Papa found reasons why it was not convenient to have them there. There was no making him happy.

Mama rented a portion of our next home to Eustace and Juliana Lee. While they lived with us, they had two children, Kevin and Kerry, for whom Mama became a surrogate grandmother. When Mama was not busy building houses, she cared for Kevin and Kerry when their parents were not available.

Papa continued to create a problem for Mama. His tantrums, cruelty, and physical abuse almost drove her to insanity. On one occasion she ripped the clothes she had on, only to forget doing so afterward. On another occasion I saw her sit on the edge of the tub, as if she was about to wash her feet. Instead, she lay back, apparently mistakenly believing she was on her bed. As she tumbled she hit her head on the side of the tub. That almost drove me over the edge.

On another occasion, she held on to me while hitting me. I was confused because I had done nothing wrong. Papa cried out to me, "Get away, can't you see she's crazy?" I broke free but I was torn because I wanted to go back and hold her to calm her. She collapsed onto the bed exhausted and soon fell asleep, breathing very heavily. Many times afterward, whenever she slept during the day, I worried that she would die. I routinely sat on the floor beside the bed and watched her chest closely, waiting to see its movement to tell me she was breathing and still alive. Her mental state improved as she called upon her inner strength to carry her through her struggles. Otherwise, I am sure she would have been committed to an insane asylum. This was a very difficult period in her life.

Papa's cousin, Fuk Tai Goo, convinced Papa to leave home for a short time, hoping to give Mama a break. Yet, that did not stop his tormenting behavior. While he did not live with us, he stalked Mama and our family. One night, as I happened to look out a window, I saw this face staring at me. I thought I'd seen a ghost and I started screaming. It was Papa. He conveyed to Mama that he was going to kill himself and the entire family in the new house that she was building.

She decided to accept him back into the home, and she disclosed to me many years later, that she fully believed he would have carried through on his threats. She wasn't afraid of dying, but she could not live with the idea of her children being killed. Consequently, she made up her mind to sacrifice her life to ensure that she brought us up in the right way to become respectful citizens of the world. I'm happy to say in that respect she succeeded.

There were still altercations, and I found myself in the middle of one. Being the youngest of my siblings, I was the one usually around when the altercations occurred. A realtor had just shown our home for sale to a prospective buyer, and Papa had interfered and suggested a ridiculously low sale price. After the agent and the prospective buyer left, Mama took Papa to task that he could have lost her the sale and why did he even say anything when he had no idea what he was talking about. Papa was incensed that she dared to question him. He lunged forward to attack her. I felt it was my duty to protect her and I jumped right in between them and shoved him away. This allowed Mama to put some distance between them and I backed away. Papa became even angrier and he picked up his board slipper and threw it at me. I dodged the slipper, picked it up, and threw it back at him, hitting him in his chest. I ran into my room and locked the door. He ran outside, turned on the garden hose and sprayed water through the open window at me. I quickly closed the window and waited for him to cool off, while keeping my ear attuned to ensure Mama was not in harm's way.

Mama did whatever was required to be done. I accompanied her one day on her travel to the Jake Street property she was in the process of building. I was eleven years old and I was embarrassed. Her shortcut to the property entailed climbing down into a man-made gully, climbing up the other side, and walking across the dump to get to a road that eventually led her to the property. She was overweight but that did not stop her since it saved time and money to take that route.

She was often deep in thought and when I asked what the matter was, she would simply say she was calculating. I knew that she was extremely stressed. Many times I accompanied her on long bus rides in the evening. She never spoke, and I was afraid to interrupt her thoughts. She just stared out the window. I sometimes became worried when we got to the end of the line when it was dark and she appeared uncertain where we were. We usually just took the return trip, and after maybe an hour, she seemed to be herself again. On those bus rides, I knew she needed me there even if I didn't speak and couldn't protect her. She had always been there for us and I wanted to be there for her. At other times she and I went to see a Chinese film at Ward Theatre. I did not really understand the movie. But it seemed to bring her enjoyment, and I was only too happy to accompany her because eventually she tended to be more relaxed. I was deeply worried for her and I did not know how I could help. I had no one I could speak to about this except in my silent prayers to God. I asked him to keep her well and alive because I knew we would all be lost without her.

In 1975, Mama decided that she could no longer stay in Jamaica. There were uprisings against anyone who was not black. There was a particular real threat against the Chinese. This situation had been precipitated by an incident in which a Chinese baker reportedly physically attacked one of his pregnant female employees. It was an excuse for angry blacks who felt they were oppressed to rise up against the Chinese who had come to Jamaica and "stolen" their money. They could not accept that the reason for the success of the Chinese was that in general the Chinese were entrepreneurial and willing to work hard. Mama decided to go to Hong Kong to live. She felt there was nowhere else to go. Vincent was in Spain, Violet was in New York, Sterling was in Toronto, and I and my husband and my children were in the process of applying to migrate to Toronto. Violet had begun the application to sponsor her to the United States but since Mama knew no one in New York and could not speak English, Mama envisioned herself sitting at home staring at the walls if she moved to New York. Mama asked Vi to discontinue the application.

Spain was not an option either for similar reasons. She had not considered Toronto at the time. She sold the triplex where she and Papa were living and where she had two other tenants. Although she had no papers permitting her to live in Hong Kong, because she was a citizen of Jamaica, she moved to Hong Kong since she felt safer there. She did not abandon Papa, although she could have. En route to Hong Kong she stopped in Canada and invested her life's savings in Toronto. Mama took just enough funds to live on in Hong Kong. The account was placed in her name as well as in my sister Violet's and my name. She trusted us.

I had accompanied her to Miami where she collected her money from the bank where we had been making deposits over the years. We flew from Miami to New York, where we met Violet and together we flew to Toronto. It was priceless to see Mama's reaction to the cold air as she exited the airport building and quickly shrunk back from the cold. She could not believe how cold it was. Violet had brought her a spring coat but it was not enough to warm her. When we got into the airport limousine to make our way to the hotel, Mama remarked how warm it was in the cab, much to the amusement of my sister Vi, who was quite used to the colder climate in the north, having lived in New York for several years. While in Toronto we stayed at the Sheraton Hotel for a couple of days so that Mama could do her banking and connect to her flight out to Hong Kong via Vancouver. We did not do very much in Toronto but Mama said it was the happiest she had ever been, because of having Violet and me with her. I had been able to get a discounted rate for the hotel because of being employed by a travel agency in Jamaica. Our room overlooked the new Toronto City Hall and Mama enjoyed looking out of the window, watching people walk to and fro.

Mama and me in Toronto

Vi and I went out to a nearby Chinese Restaurant to pick up some takeout food for supper and Mama reported watching us walk back toward the hotel. Amazing how a simple meal eaten out of foil containers could be so enjoyable. Vi and I were here to send Mama off on another life adventure. We did not really know what would be awaiting her at the other end, but Mama was so resolute on her decision. She had reasoned that this was the best alternative for her, and we did not question her plans. We had long ago learned that Mama was a very resourceful and wise person, and we simply supported her as much as we could.

A Toronto firefighters strike was on, and the larger aircrafts were not permitted to fly out of the Toronto airport. Violet and I caught a shuttle bus to Buffalo to catch our flights back to New York, while Mama was rerouted on another smaller aircraft from Toronto via Vancouver. When we waved goodbye to her at the departure gate, forgetting for a few minutes all the incredible things she had managed to do thus far, we worried how she would manage with her limited understanding of the English language.

When she arrived in Hong Kong, she stayed with friends for a short while until she bought a condo in Tai Po in the New Territories and furnished it. Not having any status in Hong Kong, she purchased the condo in her nephew's name. Mama was blessed that her nephew was a very ethical person and did not use this to his advantage. Papa joined Mama once she had a place for him to live. Mama was still Mary Lee the builder, as she decided to convert the one bedroom condo to a two bedroom apartment unit by incorporating the balcony space. Mama and Papa were living off of the money she'd taken to Hong Kong with her, along with extra cash from a little work she also did. She was engaged in turning gloves that had been sewn on the inside to right-side out. She was a frugal woman and she credited her life to God. She believed fully that she would not have survived those very turbulent and violent years without relying on God. She believed firmly that with God everything was possible. It was then no wonder that when she decided that she needed to once again pull up roots, she was able to do so.

A New Life in Toronto

In about 1982, I was able to sponsor Mama and Papa to move to Toronto, where I lived. Mama led what seemed to be a normal life in Toronto insofar as having friends and being able to manage financially. However, Papa continued to exercise control over her. She no sooner went to visit friends when he demanded that she return home immediately. It appeared he had stopped gambling and had become too old to continue his carousing. He continued, however, to be abusive, but in less obvious ways.

Mama had attended church throughout her life ever since she was first invited to the Roman Catholic Church. When she lived in Tai Po she lived right across from a Catholic Church, and she worshipped there. When she came to Canada she continued to go to a Catholic church. Eventually she found a Chinese Baptist Church in which she could at last understand what was being said. It also helped that they had fellowship Sundays at least once a month. Papa berated her for her belief in God, but Mama ignored him and continued to read her Bible every single day. Papa openly willed the vehicle transporting Mama and several other seniors to church services to overturn and kill "all those stupid women." His remarks were vitriolic and mean. Mama was typically able to ignore him until one day she said, "I need to move away from this, I can't take it anymore." I shared this with Violet, and when Violet called to discuss it with Mama, Papa overheard on the phone extension. When he learned that Mama had planned to leave him, Papa began to sharpen a cleaver as he told her that he intended to kill her if she attempted to leave. At the old age of eighty, she was still being controlled and threatened by this villain, this ungrateful tyrant. Nonetheless, Mama consoled herself with the fact that all her children were grown up, they appeared to be in control of their lives, and they were doing well. Knowing that she had accomplished her goal, she resigned herself to live out her few remaining years with him.

Her one unfulfilled desire was to see her son Vincent once more before she died. In 1987 she and I traveled to Alicante, Spain, to reunite with Vincent. It is hard to even imagine what thoughts and emotions

Mama was experiencing when she was finally able to see Vincent after more than twenty-seven years. Mama and Vincent held hands as if they were long lost lovers. I was actually glad that a relationship breakup had made me want to get away and provided me this opportunity to grant Mama's long-awaited wish.

A Life of Struggle Ends in Struggle

On May 10, 1989, Mama had been in agony all day, but it was only later in the day, when I received a call from Papa, that I learned she was not well. Upon my arrival at their apartment, Papa was waiting for me by the side entrance. When I ran up the stairs and entered the apartment and saw Mama writhing across the bed in agony, I was angry that Papa had left her alone and had not called me earlier. The paramedics came quickly. I gave no thought to Papa as I jumped into the ambulance to be with Mama, and a fifteen-minute ride seemed like forever. I so wanted her to be free of pain.

At the hospital she begged me to be put her out of her misery. I simply could not make that decision myself. When I spoke to Violet on the phone and related to her the opinion of the surgeon, we both decided we had to give her the chance to live, and so I consented to the surgery.

It was a mere six years earlier that she had been diagnosed as having an aneurism. She was told at the time that if the aneurism ever erupted it was likely she would die. She refused to have the surgery at that time, stating that she had lived a long life already and she was ready to meet her maker.

While she was in surgery for the aneurism in her aorta, I telephoned Papa to inform him of the situation. I blew a gasket when all he said to me was that she had some money on her and her ring. Twenty three years later I am able to reflect and think perhaps he was just at a loss as to what to say. However, years of living with a father who was self-absorbed and cruel to my mother did not permit me to be so forgiving at the time. I was even angrier when my brother Sterling arrived at the hospital and immediately inquired whether Mama had a will. I had to go outside to prevent myself from exploding. Her well being was top of mind for me, not what would happen to her estate. I think Sterling and his wife Maria soon realized that it was an inappropriate time to raise the subject, and apologized when I reentered the hospital.

I was not allowed to see Mama after the lengthy surgery that had extended into the early morning, and the hospital sent me home to rest. Shortly after I got into bed, I received a call to return to the hospital. They had resuscitated Mama several times and they felt there was no point in doing so again because there was irreparable damage to her liver and other organs. After I consulted with my sister Violet, I gave the go-ahead for the hospital not to resuscitate Mama.

Mama led a life of pain and struggle and her death was in pain and struggle. By contrast, two years after her death Papa passed away apparently peacefully in his sleep. I would like to think that he came to regret how he had treated Mama.

Chapter 3

Every Goal Has a Price

Who Are We to Judge?

It must have been difficult for you to read about Mama's life without wondering why she suffered her circumstances when it appeared she did not have to do so. I wondered that myself, but she had explained that she firmly believed that if she left Papa, he would have carried through on his threats to kill her and their children. Were there other ways she could have dealt with this situation? Perhaps, but who are we to judge when we did not live her reality?

Our Upbringing and Beliefs Don't Have to Control Us

How we live our lives—how we act—are shaped in large part by our upbringing and our beliefs. Sometimes these beliefs protect us. Sometimes they serve to our disadvantage.

As you saw, Mama's cultural background led her to believe that females had no value and were subservient to men. Her upbringing also placed a lot of store in having little control over one's destiny, and her faith did not condone divorce. Despite those beliefs, Mama determined and decided what her purpose in life was, and it was so huge and important that it gave her the strength to withstand severe hardships and she found the courage to embark on undertakings unimagined as possible for an uneducated, illiterate Chinese woman.

The Goal and the Price

Mama's main goal for her life was to keep us children safe from harm and to provide for us so that we could grow up to be self-sufficient, decent, and responsible adults. She kept that goal in the forefront of her mind, and everything she did was a step toward that goal. If something didn't support her goal, she dismissed it. No price was too much to pay to achieve her goal—and did she ever pay that price! Some may think she paid too high a price. Mama didn't think so. Toward the end of her life, she said, "I am satisfied."

Ask her children whether we appreciated what she did for us and the answer is a resounding "yes." I am so grateful, in fact, that I want to live the rest of my life ensuring that the price she paid is richly rewarded, and that if she can look down from heaven she can eventually say, "I am so proud of Rose and yes, the price I paid was worth it."

Handle Problems with Prayer

What opportunities have you been given because someone made a sacrifice for you?

Mama believed in the power of prayer and always gave credit to God for her accomplishments. Her credo was "Without God I am nothing, with God I can do anything if that is His Will." So many people go to God and tell Him how big their storms are. Instead we should tell our storms how big our God is.

Mama had no one to coach her but she figured it out for herself. When she faced circumstances she decided were not to her liking, she did not cripple herself by blaming anyone or feeling sorry for herself. Instead, she decided what she wanted for her life, she determined what she had to do to achieve her goals, and she did exactly that, without hesitation.

When she faced a stumbling block, she simply handled it with prayer.

Mama always trusted that the solution would show itself if she stood back away from the problems and accepted the gifts hidden in them.

What Are Your Challenges?
What Will You Do about Them?

I hope you will be inspired by Mama's story. No doubt you are reading this book, so you are educated. You may have limiting cultural beliefs, but the world has become such a big place. We are more advanced and more tolerant. You may have no funds now, but there are more avenues to finding funds than there were in Mama's day. You will have your moral values challenged in this ever-permissive world, but remaining true to who you really are will provide less stress in your life and also in your body. If you have a dream, believe it is within your power to achieve it, and take action. As various successful people have observed, *"If the mind can conceive it, and your heart can believe it, then you can achieve it."*

Let Mama be an example that no matter what you've been taught, no matter what your circumstances, no matter who is in your life, you can accomplish your dream. You will have to be clear of course about your big purpose in life, realize that there is a price to be paid for everything and decide whether your purpose is important enough and worth the price that will be extracted for its accomplishment.

Summary

- Cultural influences, lack of education, lack of money, your life partner, other people's expectations, or language barriers are not barriers to your success.
- Examine your situation. If it's not acceptable, decide what it is you wish instead.
- Know where you want to be and what your goals are.
- Determine whether you are willing to pay the price to accomplish your goals.
- Figure what needs to be done to reach your goals.
- Take action.
- Handle your problems with prayer.
- When you're given an idea, the way will show itself.

Chapter 4

When You're Gone, What Will Be Said about You?

I READ SOMEWHERE THAT WE SHOULD imagine what we want to be said about us at our funeral and commence to live our lives accordingly. We are in effect leaving a legacy for our children, our family, friends, and the world at large. I do believe we all have a mandate to leave this world a better place because we were here. Are you living your life with authenticity and in service?

I am not proposing that you give up your wealth, join the monastery, or become like Mother Teresa. Every day we interact with people—our spouse, our children, our clients, our employees, our fellow workers, our bosses, our friends, our colleagues, the store clerk, the gas attendant, the coffee shop server, the cleaning person, the garbage truck driver, and others. When you can honestly answer that your interaction with these individuals added to their lives in a positive way and you focus on doing that every day, your world will shift immeasurably. Allow yourself to see the good in others.

Try this for ninety days until it becomes a habit.

What I Wish I Had Said at Mama's Funeral

I was too grief stricken to think of giving a eulogy at Mama's funeral, but it has now been twenty-three years since her passing. People who have been very influential in our lives may physically leave us, but they continue to be a very integral part of our lives. I recall thinking on the occasion of my call to the Bar, *I wish Mama was here to see me become a lawyer*, only to quickly rationalize that I would not have wanted her to live through my trials and tribulations prior to that significant event. When faced with challenges, I remind myself that my situation is not as dire compared to Mama's circumstances. In recalling Mama's indomitable spirit, I am able to find the inner strength I need to deal with my situation.

Here is what I feel should be said about Mama:

Mama was influenced by her culture, by her beliefs in destiny, and by her views on marriages lasting forever. She was led to believe females had no use or value, and no doubt some of her choices in life were governed by those same limiting beliefs. Nonetheless, she led a purpose-driven life. She defined what she wanted for her life and went after it, no matter what challenges presented themselves. **She was focused and determined.**

Mama's goal to keep her children safe and raise them to be self-sufficient adults was realized. When her goal of bringing her first child, her daughter in China, to Jamaica was possible, her daughter chose not to go to Jamaica. Mama was satisfied at any rate that she had done her part and that if her oldest daughter did not want to come, it was out of her control. Mama also repaid Mother-in-Law's debt. **She honored her commitments.**

Not only did she achieve her goals, she also demonstrated courage, perseverance, and innovative thinking while doing so. She accomplished it all, despite the many naysayers who told her, "You're crazy. What do you know? What do you mean you're going to build houses?" Although she remained married to Papa until her death and could be considered by some to have been a victim, she was anything but a victim. She had reasoned out what price she was willing to pay to accomplish her goals and she paid the price because she knew her goal was well worth having. **She was resourceful and brave.**

Chin Lim Geow/Mary Lee/Mama had a strong faith in God. She did not rebuke God for her lot in life. She simply asked Him for guidance. **She was a woman of strong faith and she was grateful for her blessings—even those that came in the guise of challenges.**

She did not let her lack of education, her gender, her cultural background, her lack of money or her dysfunctional marriage hold her back. Her belief was that if she was willing, the way will show itself. **She had a limitless approach to life.**

As a Chinese in a foreign country, an uneducated woman with no funds, married to a husband who did nothing but pull her down, she was able to say, "I need to do this, I want to do this, and I'll find a way to do it." Most importantly; she actually took action toward her goals instead of just talking about them, or worse yet, bemoaning her circumstances. **She was a pragmatic, take-action person.**

She was a good woman, she respected all, and she was generous with her time and counsel. She gave of herself and asked nothing in return.

Lim Geow, Mary Lee, Mama—you are forever cherished by everyone you left behind.

At back L-R: Donald, Sterling, Vincent. At front
L-R: Vi and Me after Mama's funeral.

What Will Be Said about You When You're Gone?

We won't really know what will be said about us when we're gone, and we have little control over other people's opinions. However, if we live our lives being true to who we really are, not who someone else wants us to be, and we accomplish the goals we set for ourselves despite adversities and actually make a positive difference in someone else's life, we are indeed living a worthy life.

What do you want to be said about you when you're gone? Will you have regrets? At the end of your days, will you be content that you were the best person you could be? Will you be able to say that you lived an authentic life? Will you be missed? My mentor, Brendon Burchard asked himself the following questions when he was in a horrible vehicle accident—*Did I live (fully)? Did I love (openly)? Did I matter?* What will you be asking yourself?

Regardless of where you are at today, now is the best time to start to live your best life. Rome was not built in a day, and the only way you can eat an elephant is one bite at a time.

Take your first step now—**a journey of a thousand miles starts with a single step**. Find a kindred spirit to accompany you on your walk. They may not accompany you all the way, but at each step of your journey you will find the help you need when you need it. I am grateful to you for allowing me to spend some time with you at this step of your journey.

It's not too late. Start now. (Well, at least after you finish reading this book.)

Summary

- Imagine what you wish to be said about you at your funeral and live your life accordingly.
- We all have a mandate to leave this world a better place because we were here.
- Live your life being true to who you really are, not who someone else wants you to be.
- Accomplish your goals despite adversities.
- Make a positive difference in someone else's life.
- Start to live your best life today.

Chapter 5

Lessons Learned—My Story

Early Days

I BEGAN TO EXPLORE MY OUTSIDE world by holding on to the railing of the porch surrounding the old house located behind the grocery store at Victoria Street. This was how I learned to walk under the watchful eye of Stella. Stella was an average-looking black woman whom Mama hired to take care of the children and to wash, iron, and clean.

Stella washed our clothes by hand in a metal wash basin and hung them on a line to dry. She swept, mopped, and polished the old wooden floors. To polish the floors, she got down on her knees and used a brush made from a dried coconut cut in half. The bristles worked really well to bring out the shine. By the time she finished the floors, the clothes had dried in the hot Jamaica sun. It was time to iron them.

Stella carefully lit the big chunks of coal in the little black stove with a match and a little piece of rolled up newspaper. When the coals were glowing red and hot, she placed several black cast irons directly onto the coals to heat. (Who said it's bad to have many irons in the fire?) She picked up one of the irons, carefully cleaned its surface with a piece of pork fat, and followed this with a quick, careful rub of a clean cloth before using it to iron. As soon as one iron lost its heat, she placed it back over the coals, selecting another. She repeated the process until the clothes were all ironed. Pretty much all our clothes needed ironing since they were made from cotton.

While I would observe Stella, she would observe me. I was always aware of her watchful eye on me. Amazingly, she invariably found time away from her chores to come and amuse me.

Stella created a type of toy that made a whirring sound. She took an old button with two holes, through which she looped and tied a piece of thread. She held an end of the thread with each of her hands, twirled the button around several times loosely, and pulled the thread taut to create a whirring sound as the button spun back. By bringing her hands closer together and apart, just as if playing an accordion, this whirring sound continued, seemingly endlessly, to my utter delight. Stella sometimes did this close to Sterling's ear in order to awaken him from his nap. She made me an accomplice in her antics by signaling with her finger to her lips for me to keep quiet as she snuck up on him.

As I grew tired, I crawled into the huge metal wash basin lined with pillows to have a nap.

When my brothers and sister would return home from school, I would be in heaven. I was not alone any more. Even though Stella was there, I knew instinctively she was not my family. My siblings amused me. My sister Vi entertained me with her love of dance and song. I joined in at age three, and she and I pranced around with our thumbs up in the air, singing

Thumbelina, Thumbelina tiny little thing
Thumbelina dance, Thumbelina sing
Thumbelina what's the difference if you're very small?
When your heart is full of love you're nine feet tall.

It was a cute little song and it told me that **love is important**.

Songs, movies—anything we listen to or read—all influence our subconscious mind, and we should **exercise more discernment about what we expose ourselves to each day.**

You Don't Always Get What You Ask For

We did not have traditional toys, and our imaginations transformed sand into sugar, dirt into flour, and rocks into bread, potatoes, or yams as we played "shop." We used empty tin cans and jar lids as measuring cups or plates. Little pebbles were coins, and leaves were paper money. My older siblings used a piece of lumber as a cricket bat, and little stones wrapped carefully with a generous amount of cloth and string became the cricket ball. I believe that was Vincent's idea. During one such game, I got into the middle and was hit with a stray ball. It knocked me out cold, and the older children panicked, shaking me vigorously and calling my name in order to revive me. For a minute or so I heard nothing, but I revived immediately after the enticing question of "Do you want a Coca-Cola" was asked. Of course, I answered "yes." I have been accused of having faked my concussion but I can honestly say I did not. I did not get that Coca-Cola, and it was possibly the first of many broken promises in my life. I learned **you don't always get what you ask for or are promised.**

Serve to Receive Love and Appreciation

I had learned to be obedient (not to speak unless spoken to) and to please people—even to please Papa. At age three, I learned a little Chinese ditty:

Ham nyi chong go, Nyi chu chong,
chong chut nyit tey dui nyet gong,
chong chut kee ling dui fung fong.

This was its translation:

Ask me to sing a song, I will soon sing,
sing until the sun meets the moon,
sing until the dragon meets the red room.

Papa delighted in asking me to recite this in front of friends and asking me to show them my *nee git* (ears), *nyan* (eyes), *tey la huk* (head).

I deduced that to get any appreciation I needed to do whatever it took to make others happy. I was often praised by Papa and Mama. At less than five years old, I took the empty soda bottles around to the back, behind the shop, and put them into the crates for pickup by the soda company delivery truck. Consequently, I learned that **initiative and work are praiseworthy qualities.** It felt good to be praised, and I grew up always wanting to be praised and appreciated.

Did you know that 95 percent of our programming comes from our childhood? My childhood experiences programmed me to believe that in order to be appreciated and to receive what I interpreted to be affection, I had to be a good girl and be helpful. It would be years later before I realized I needed to change my programming in order to have a mature adult relationship. In the Chinese culture, at least back then, affection was never openly given. It was a long time before I understood that Mama loved me. She had never hugged me and never said she loved me. In my adult years, she even criticized me for showing too much affection for my children too openly, and she told me that I loved my children too much. I imagine that from Mama's perspective, she did not wish for me the same fate that she had: sacrificing everything for her children. I knew what I had missed as a child, however, and I was not going to deny my children the affection that I had yearned for. The lack of affection in my younger years left an emptiness in me, and that emptiness led me to look for love in all the wrong places.

I grew up craving affection, and it took me a long time to realize that **I have to love myself and not depend on others to love me.**

Be Thankful

Growing up, I also understood that I needed to appreciate having food on the table, no matter how simple or ordinary it was. Mama celebrated very simple meals that she was able to afford. We always had lots of rice, but what accompanied the rice was sometimes as little and simple as a duck egg. We were fortunate if we got half an egg. It was a preserved (salted) duck egg and its shell was coated with black ash. The black ash had to be removed from around the shell, and the egg was washed and then either boiled or cooked in its shell with the rice. We often crushed the duck egg to distribute the saltiness and flavor into the rice. I'm not so sure there was a lot of nutritional value, but it sure was good. If we were still hungry, we ate more rice. This part was made more appealing when we were able to scrape the rice off the sides and bottom of the pot to form a little rice ball, sprinkle it with soya sauce, and devour it all at once. Another dish we enjoyed was fish (kingfish), which Mama had salted thoroughly and wrapped with cord in newspaper and hung to dry for countless days in the sun. Because of its saltiness, it went a long way when we had it with rice, so there was no need to have more than a very small piece. Chinese sausage was another staple we had. It was steamed atop the rice, and again, cut into small pieces. We sometimes were fortunate to get a whole one, but typically, as we were children, a half of a sausage was all we got. There was almost always stir fried greens (spinach, bok choy, or even sometimes lettuce that was too wilted to eat fresh). Regardless of how basic or how little our meals were, Mama always gave thanks for what we had before us.

We never felt deprived, even though we instinctively knew we had very little money. We also knew there could be a lot more, because Mama did on occasion have a special meal with more than two or three dishes. This was typically around Chinese New Year or Christmas. It was considered bad manners to sing at the table, and if we did so, Mama said we were behaving "beggar-like." Any transgressions received a *"gat chuk"*—a rap with the knuckle to the head. When food was placed in front of us, we ate, never refusing to eat something because we didn't like it—that was unmannerly and demonstrated ungratefulness. We were reminded not to reach across to parts of the dishes away from us just because we wanted a better piece of chicken or meat. To encourage us to clean our plates, Mama told us if we left anything on our plates, even a grain of rice, our future spouse was sure to have a bumpy face. Although we tried to be careful not to waste food, shoveling rice into our mouths from the rice bowls with our chopsticks would sometimes result in rice grains going astray, falling onto the floor to be later swept up with a broom after the meal.

Mama gave thanks every time she sat down to eat. She didn't command us to pray, she led by example as she bowed her head, made the sign of the cross, and silently gave thanks.

We wore hand-me-downs from other families or from an older brother or sister who had already had the benefit of the clothing. This did not detract from our pleasure of having "new" used clothing to wear. New clothing was a rare occurrence, but as things improved, Mama always made sure that my sister Vi and I each had a new dress (usually matching in style and color) at Christmastime, especially sewn for us by a dressmaker. The boys also got new clothing. Otherwise, Vi and I wore clothes made from bags that previously held chicken feed or cornmeal. From my childlike perspective, they were pretty. I loved the ones with the delicate little flower patterns. Yes we were poor, but we learned to **be thankful for what we had.**

Inferiority Complex

Mama talked often about some of our distant cousins. She spoke about how smart they were, that they had graduated high school, and that they were working. She recounted all the wonderful accomplishments they had achieved. Some of them received scholarships and went off to college. I knew it wasn't just because they were smart; it was also because their parents had enough money to send them to college. Although we were not being directly compared, I heard enough praises for these cousins that I couldn't help but feel inferior to them. Despite my not being the brightest spark, I somehow managed to complete preparatory school (elementary school) and to receive a scholarship placement to an all-girls high school—Alpha Academy High School for Girls, also known as Convent of Mercy Academy. My tuition was free, but the costs of my books and uniforms were not included. I am still amazed that I was able to do this, because frankly, I found school terribly confusing.

Classes, of course, were conducted in English. Although I understood English, my first language was Chinese, as spoken in my home. That Chinese, however, was a dialect called *Hakka*. It is not one of the mainstream dialects of China. Consequently, when people would expect me to speak Chinese with them, I would have to disappoint them. Chinese kids of my generation who grew up in Jamaica were called "bananas"—yellow on the outside and white on the inside. We were also called *Ah Lem* (dumb—unable to speak) if we could not speak Chinese.

School was difficult not only because of the language but also because I had no one to help me with my homework. Neither of my parents wrote, read, or spoke English, except for a few words they could speak to customers of their shops. My parents did not understand what was being taught or what was expected of us. Even if Papa had understood, he would likely not have been interested to assist me. As a result, I always felt disadvantaged. Surprisingly, I did get through high school and graduated—not at the top of the class, but I nonetheless made it. Of course, when parent permission was required, my siblings and I simply signed Mama's name. The teachers never met Mama or Papa, and as well as I can remember we did not have parent-teacher meetings. How lucky for kids today that their parents are called to be involved with their education!

Well-meaning adults sometimes talk about the accomplishments of others only in an attempt to inspire young children to aim higher. **If the child is somewhat insecure, comparisons with other children can only serve to feed an inferiority complex. It is better to encourage them to be the best they can be without comparing them to others.** Personally, I teetered between feeling inferior and wanting to do better.

Choose Your Friends Wisely

In elementary school, there were girls that I chummed around with. We took to going to a thrift store that was a short walking distance from school, and it soon became evident that a couple of the girls were shoplifting. As much as I knew it was wrong, I didn't want to lose my place among "friends" and I became complicit in the outings. **Peer pressure can be overwhelming. Sometimes, the need to be accepted can be in total conflict with your values.**

Thankfully, one day a group of them came home with me and when Mama discovered this, she banned me from associating with them. Mama had an uncanny gift of accurately reading a person's character within a short period of time. At school, I was still their friend, but I stopped associating with them outside of school. My mother's acceptance was more important to me and so was feeling that I was true to my values.

Mama had warned me not to go into any one's home, and I was not permitted to invite anyone home. I did not always heed her warning; sometimes I did sneak off to a schoolmate's home after school. I reasoned that there really was no harm, since Shelly Deidrich's home was not far away and her mother made me feel very welcome. Susan Chin's home held a wonderful world of books, and I dove into them whenever I visited. Aesop's Fables reminded me of the wonderful parables Mama spoke about. I rationalized: *How could that be wrong?*

Although Mama was a kind person, she was also mistrustful. One of her beliefs was that we should associate only with people better than we were. Vi was quick to point out to her that if those people who were better than we were did the same thing, then they would not want to associate with us. I have since learned, however, that we cannot continue to associate with negative people who do nothing but drag us down or keep us back. **We need to associate with people who will motivate and inspire us to become better individuals.** Wealth gurus have proposed that you can tell what a person's level of income is by the incomes of the six other people with whom that person associates.

When Mama lived above the warehouse at Luke Lane, the gentleman who ran the warehouse, Mr. Lue, brought his daughter along with him, and we became playmates very quickly. Elsie was cute, and I longed to have her long flowing hair, which she always wore in a ponytail. Also, she had a caring father who obviously catered to her desires. For some reason, Elsie and I ended up in a play tussle and she knocked out one of my rotting teeth. The candies from Mama's previous store and the lack of dental hygiene had taken their toll. I quickly rinsed out my mouth and decided I had not deserved to have my tooth knocked out. I proceeded to exact my revenge. Elsie went crying to her dad to report how I had knocked out her tooth, only to be met with a rebuke that she must have provoked me because I would not have done that without a reason. I confess I did not get any satisfaction for my revenge, but it was an important step for me to know that if I were pushed too far, I could stand up for myself. **Children can learn their tolerance limit by experience.**

Elsie and I lost touch when Mama moved our family away to her next venture, but we reconnected when we were in high school and again recently. **Some friends will always remain friends despite the passing of time or distance.**

Circumstances Teach Resourcefulness or Lessons

I had not yet begun school when we first moved to Luke Lane. One day, Mama had to run out very quickly, and she left me alone at home with the admonition to stay inside and not let anyone in. I grew impatient for her to return, left the apartment, and went down the stairs to sit at the door to wait for her. The door, which was on a spring hinge, slammed shut, leaving me locked outdoors. I went to the bar next door to get help but also partly out of curiosity to see this place where patrons gathered at night to enjoy the blaring jukebox. Night after night the musical sounds of "She-erry, Sherry baby" floated through our apartment window, along with "One two three, look at Mr. Lee; three, four, five, look at him jive, Mr. Lee, Mr. Lee, oh Mr. Lee." My childlike fleeting impression told me that this place was not the attraction, but rather it was the people who came there each night that gave life to the place. I told them what had happened and the owner took me upstairs, where his opened window looked directly across to our opened window. There was only two to three feet of space between them. He placed a plank in between the windows and I crawled across on my hands and knees to safety.

Upon Mama's return, I proudly told her how I had solved my problem. She was aghast and informed me that I had now made it obvious how someone could easily gain access to our home. Frankly, I rather like to think it was the beginning of my resourcefulness, although in hindsight I can see how I could easily have come to harm.

Shortly after we moved there, my brother Donald one evening made what I thought was a logical conclusion. He told Mama that there were two moons, one at Victoria Street and one at Luke Lane where we now were. Mama laughed, and **I learned that things are not always what they seem.**

Donald ventured out onto the roof of a building to the south of our apartment, and not wanting to be left out, I followed after him. The building was a soda bottling plant, and we took turns looking through missing-nail holes on the roof to see the activity on the plant floor. Mama caught us and scolded us for climbing out onto the roof. I must have been disrespectful, since Mama became angry, took her left hand and lifted my chin and with the other hand slapped me across my face. I was speechless, and although it hurt, I cried very silently because I knew I was out of order and I had been reminded.

Although I do not condone physical discipline, I believe today's parents are too afraid to take charge or to set boundaries, thus letting children believe that the children are in control. Consequently, children do not respect parental authority.

Physical discipline was seldom if ever used by Mama, and when she slapped me she must have been under much stress at the time. She, however, knew better than to apologize for slapping me. I knew it hurt her to slap me but she held her ground and the lesson was learned. **Parents are not to be shown disrespect.**

Disciplining a child is not easy but it must be done in a firm, responsible manner for the child's own good.

When You're Not in Charge

When I started school, my bamboo lunch pail was my prized possession. Lunch consisted of two tablespoons of condensed milk mixed with a glass of water as my drink, along with a bologna or fried egg sandwich. The milk often leaked, and as it congealed and heated up in the warm temperatures, it smelled horrible. With this lunch pail, I would head out from home to school.

Donald and I walked to "Parade" now known as St. William Grant Park, which is where all the buses originated to travel in all directions in Kingston. There were so many buses and so many people that it was confusing and somewhat frightening. Donald was charged with my safety, and he made sure I stuck close with him. He was likely not more than nine years old and it must surely have been an onerous task to be saddled with one's baby sister.

At the end of the school day, he usually found me and we took the bus home together. On a few occasions he simply told me to wait while he visited with his friend or played a friendly game of football (soccer) in the school field. I knew I had no choice, so I resigned myself to waiting for him. At least I knew he always eventually got me home. Not having control, however, irked me.

On one occasion, he spent our bus fares and we had to walk for at least two hours to get home. Upon my return home, my face was beet red from the sun and exertion. Mama gave Donald a lecture about responsibility, but she was relieved we were safe and a little amused at how flushed I was. Again, I thought to myself, *When I'm old enough, I won't have to wait around for anyone or depend on anyone.* My urge to have control over my own destiny was being developed.

At our next home, 20 Gold Street, we also had to take the bus to get to school, and this time it required changing buses. My big sister Vi took me to school each day. We walked to the top of Gold Street to catch our first bus to Parade. The ten minute bus ride took us to Parade, where we caught the number 11 bus to school. One particular morning the buses were crowded and slow, and Vi decided we should walk to Parade. The road to cross over to catch the number 11 bus was extremely busy. We were halfway across, and with traffic passing us on both sides, I apparently panicked and let go of Vi's hand to run back to the sidewalk. A cyclist could not avoid striking me and I was thrown up into the air and landed on the road, causing traffic to come to a screeching halt.

When I came to, I was sitting on a roadside vendor's bench with no recollection of crossing the road or being hit. Vi was frustrated that we were even further delayed when we had already been running late. It was clear, however, that she was concerned about me. We carried on to school, but upon arriving I began to feel quite dizzy and disoriented. The priest, Father Wilson, who later became Monsignor Wilson, drove me home.

For many years I suffered from migraines, and both Mama and I surmised that it was as a result of this accident. Unfortunately my sister Vi was blamed for my accident when really it was my own fault. I had tried to take control before I was really ready. **Individuals often try to take control when they have not ascertained that they are capable of doing so.**

Actions, Deliberate or Not, Have Consequences

Various experiences as a child taught me lessons about taking responsibility for actions. One lesson involved a pair of lovely red shoes. I felt pretty grown up when Mama bought me these shoes with clunky two-inch heels, but it did not stop me from walking all over the bed with them as we often did when we had new shoes. It was a deliciously savored activity, since it was so rare to get new shoes. I carefully put them under my bed, stealing a look at them whenever I could.

One time I woke up in the middle of the night and pulled out from under the bed what I thought to be a chamber pot (chimmy) to have a pee. The chimmy was used to avoid flushing the toilet at night and avoid disturbing everyone else. I discovered in the morning that I had used my beautiful red shoes instead of the chimmy—the shoes were totally ruined. There was no money to replace them, and I suffered the consequences of my actions. This disappointment was a precursor of the many yet to come.

At 1 Trees Avenue, I would lose myself in a pretend world as my siblings and their buddies engaged in their own activities nearby.

There were various fruit trees (mango, lime, avocado, green plums, and guineps, to name a few) on the property and I entertained and had conversations with my imaginary friends in the shade of those trees while I walked about the long yard. Vincent and Sterling blocked off a bit of the yard and built an open-air gym with weights, bars to do chin lifts, and the like. Vincent provided Ovaltine and other drinks to his friends who came to lift weights. When Mama protested because of the costs, Vincent's reply was that the guys needed it to give them energy, and surprisingly Papa seemed not to mind.

Violet, Donald, and I hung around the gym area, watching the guys lift weights and clown around. We took delight in laughing at George, who was a scrawny guy who could not lift very much and had to kick like crazy when attempting to pull himself up to reach the bar with his chin. There was also Tony Chin, who, while bench pressing, dropped the weights across his throat because Vincent tickled his feet. Luckily, Tony came to no harm.

One afternoon, I had climbed into the Ackee tree, a fruit tree. I stood on the branch below the one where Donald had been standing and I placed my hand on the branch above to steady myself. Donald did not see my hand and in moving along, he kicked my hand off of the branch, sending me spiraling down to the ground, narrowly missing the rusted iron fence.

I was winded, and all I kept saying was "It's Donald fault. It's Donald's fault." I was only seven and much too young to realize that my own actions had contributed to the accident. I have since learned that **I need to take responsibility for my actions.**

No Substitute for a Good Friend

After the age of ten, I lived in a neighborhood with lots of kids around my age, and thankfully, one of them was June, a distant cousin of mine. She was more streetwise than I was. We did a lot of things together. One summer day we cycled around the neighborhood hundreds of times. June always led the way riding hands free, while I gripped my handle bars, hanging on for dear life. June taught me how to ride a bike and laughed at me each time I fell and skinned my knees—once she was sure I was fine. She was a tomboy, and we often invaded the neighborhood boys' game of soccer being played in an empty lot of land. It was not a designated park or soccer field. I think June and I liked to believe we trounced the boys at their own game or that we were the winning factor if we were on one of the boys' teams.

We did crazy things. One day we gave a Toni perm to each other's hair as well as to the hair of some of the other neighborhood girls, Joyce Yap and Janet Chin. We stunk of perm chemicals and our heads had knots of curls because we left the rollers in too long. It was a delicious day of indulgence for us as young girls, yet like many other women, I now seem to have forgotten to indulge myself for more than an hour, if at all. **As women, we need to find time for ourselves**.

June and I experimented with baking cakes and macaroni and cheese, and often we sat around just chatting. We complained about our parents. June's dad (Noel Lee Fatt, known to me as Nyuk Sang Goh) was very strict, and June felt confined, yet in my eyes she seemed to have a lot more latitude than I did. I had no complaints about Mama, but I did talk about Papa, and each time I did the tears would well up in my eyes. Many years went by before I could talk about Papa without the emotions getting the better of me.

June and I schemed about how we could get our parents to allow us to go downtown for a shopping trip. June came up with a brilliant plan. She first approached Mama with me and told Mama that she was going to go downtown to shop, and she asked Mama to allow me to accompany her. Since Mama thought that June's parents had already sanctioned the trip, Mama was agreeable to my going. Then we went to her dad, told him I was going downtown to shop, and asked if he would let June accompany me. Nyuk Sang Goh believed that since Mama had approved my going, then obviously, this must be a needed shopping trip, and he was ready to give his approval for June to accompany me. His only stipulation was that we ask for permission in Chinese.

One summer, June and I decided to have our ears pierced, and we cycled down to St. Joseph's Hospital, where the nuns did ear piercings. On our arrival, however, we were turned away, because we were not properly dressed. We were wearing shorts. This made quite an impression on me, and I have learned to **dress appropriately for each occasion**. That time, however, we were not deterred, and my sister Vi arranged for us to visit a friend of hers—Peaches Chong—who pierced our ears. She used a huge sewing needle, with thread, and had a candle to burn and sterilize the needle and ice to freeze the ear lobe. I heard the needle piercing through each layer of my ice-numbed ear. June had to be the first to have her ear pierced since she was much braver, and I followed her lead.

June and I traveled to and from school together even though we were not in the same class. June was a year and a half younger than I. We thought it was fun to walk home in a couple of downpours and were soaking, dripping wet to the point where our shoes squished as we walked. Our enjoyment was not dampened by the scolding we each received when we got home.

She was gregarious and outgoing and attracted everyone to her. I hung on to her coattails, and where she went, I went. She and her brother Lennie had spats from time to time. I could easily tell that June had the upper hand and took no nonsense from Lenny or anyone for that matter. I admired her bravado.

June and I dressed alike and even wore our hair in the same style—a high pony tail teased out to sit atop our heads. We talked about boys and life in general. One afternoon after school we consumed a whole loaf of bread between us, as each toasted, buttered slice tasted better the more we had. **There is something magical about sharing food (even toast) with a friend and sharing your innermost thoughts.**

June was very popular and I was happy to be her friend and distant cousin. **There is just no substitute for a good friend. Every woman should have at least one.**

Kids Can Be Cruel

High school life was riddled with a lot of ridicule and embarrassment. Mama did not understand that when girls are going through puberty and are beginning to show bosoms, a bra was required. In her culture, it was a shame to have large or even normal breasts. Girls were required to wrap cloth material around their breasts in order to flatten them. I have wondered—but I never asked—how my sister Violet dealt with that, since she was six years older than I. All I was aware of was that I was ridiculed and I felt mortified, especially when my classmates talked about me. They whispered behind my back. I knew what they were saying. I knew they were talking about the fact that in Phys Ed classes, and when I danced the Irish Jig in a school play, my boobs were visibly unsupported. I must admit that I wasn't too sure that there was much of anything to put into a bra at the time, but suffice it to say, I was singled out.

I was also not part of the various cliques in school. Whenever my classmates had parties or get-togethers, I was not invited. I consoled myself with the fact that even if I were invited I would not have been able to go, because Mama did not support the idea of me going out. Not that I ever asked Mama, I just knew. I just accepted my situation and did not rebel or act out.

When I was about thirteen years old, my class elected me as prefect, which is similar to a class president. I'm not sure how that came about, except I presume that my classmates might have elected me as a joke. Nonetheless, I took the responsibility that came with the position seriously and did the best I could. It took several such opportunities in my life to make me realize that I did in fact feel very comfortable in a leadership role. **Sometimes all that an individual needs is an opportunity to take a leadership position to discover she is in fact a good leader.**

In retrospect I can see that my firm belief that I was a worthwhile person, regardless of whether I was accepted, was what sustained me throughout this difficult, awkward stage. **Do not let other people's opinion of you determine your worth. You are indeed a worthwhile person.**

Finding a Safe Haven

Because of the turmoil at home and the meanness from my fellow students, I sought solace with God. My classmates mockingly referred to me as Sister Rose or Saint Rose. For some reason I had an inner peace that allowed me to ignore the taunts. I found solace in going into the chapel at lunchtime to talk to God, just to share my feelings. At the time, I didn't know how to really cope except through my conversations with God. Even though we were all caught up in the same drama, my siblings and I never discussed our situation. In retrospect, I have come to realize that **individuals all interpret and deal with events differently. It is *not* what happens to you that is important; it is how you deal with what happens to you.**

The Memorable Adolescent Years

During my teenage years I was only able to go to a party when my brother Donald was also invited. Usually it was a birthday party at the home of a teenager, and his or her parent would be in attendance to keep an eye on the kids. The beverage of choice was rum punch, a strong alcoholic beverage made of four parts water, three parts syrup, two parts over proof rum, and one part lime juice. We also had soda pops. No one ever got drunk or behaved horribly. There was just a lot of dancing and plain old fun. A meal was usually served at around 10:00 p.m. on flimsy white paper plates, with a plastic fork, followed by the birthday cake. Donald and I invariably teased each other after the parties, commenting on how the other had been "renting a tile"—the description for dancing close to someone and hardly moving.

My Sundays involved going to church in the morning with Mama, Violet, and Donald and then in the afternoon losing myself in the many books I had borrowed from the school library. They were typically classics or about the lives of saints.

About every three weeks I went to a matinee with my brother. I paid for the movie from whatever little money I had been able to save from the lunch money Mama had given to me. Since I could not go alone and Donald was not a saver, ultimately I had to pay for him to accompany me.

We took sandwiches and drinks to school for lunch, but when Mama was involved in building houses it was easier for her to give us money for lunch since she left very early in the morning for the building site. Lunch was fairly cheap, and two shillings and six pence went a long way. Oftentimes, lunch consisted of a patty and coco bread and a soda (cream soda and kola champagne were my favorites). The Jamaican beef patty had a hamburger meat filling and a tasty crust. On Fridays during Lent, when we were expected to abstain from meat, tri-cornered curried lobster patties were substituted for the beef patties. They were so delicious; it made it very easy to adhere to the Lenten practice of abstaining from meat. The coco bread was pretty heavy and could be opened to place the patty inside of it to make a sandwich. Whenever I wanted to save some money for the movies, I did without the coco bread or the drink.

As insignificant as it seems, that lesson has kept me moving forward. Yes, there is a lesson to be learned from everything. You need only look for it. The lesson is this: **when you want a desired outcome, you need to determine how you are going to accomplish that outcome and do what is necessary to get it, and it usually entails a price to be paid.** In this situation, the effort I made to save part of my lunch money was a small price to pay for the pleasure of getting dressed up, going to the movies, and escaping from reality for a couple of hours!

One of our most favorite movies was *It's a Mad Mad Mad Mad World*, where we laughed from beginning to end. It's a good movie to laugh at and to forget all your problems if even only for a short while. **Humor is a great diversion from a heavy heart.**

Influenced by Nuns and Teachers

At Alpha Academy High School I was fortunate to have the guidance of a couple of nuns and teachers who led me into charitable works—giving to the needy and serving others. One Saturday each month, I went to the school location to ration out powdered corn meal to individuals who were evidently in need. The corn meal was provided by UNICEF, and we were told how many scoops to give to each person who brought their tin cans to receive the rations. I remember thinking how grateful I was not to be in their position. **No matter how desperate your situation, if you look around there are others who are more disadvantaged than you are.**

On two afternoons each week after school, I also taught Math and English to girls in the orphanage, some of whom were older than I. It felt awkward being called "teacher" but it gave me a certain sense of satisfaction that I was actually doing something worthwhile. It also gave me confidence to share my knowledge. I have since learned that **no matter where you are on your journey, there are others who can benefit from your knowledge.**

On Sundays, I again went to school in the early afternoon to meet up with a couple of nuns to be driven to a poorer neighborhood to teach Sunday school to underprivileged kids. I still recall to this day the two little black boys who were twins—Peter and Paul. One of them came up to me and said, "Teacher, I want to go to church but I have no shoes." I am uncertain where the wisdom came from within me as I answered "It's okay to go to church even though you have no shoes; God will understand." Perhaps this memory plagues me because I am wishing I could have done something about that situation. I hope Peter and Paul were eventually able to have shoes and a better life.

In the summer holidays, I also taught summer classes to these children. Donald did as well. I now understand that this was more for my benefit than for theirs. I have come to realize that there is perhaps no true form of altruism; we all do something for others because it satisfies a need in us. The need could just be the feeling of satisfaction you get for having done something good. I was not only doing something worthwhile but also it fed my need to be appreciated. Today, I also know that **the best way to stop feeling sorry for oneself is to give to others.**

Despite taking leadership roles, I continued to be exceptionally shy. The thought of even answering a question in class in front of my classmates made my knees weak and sent the blood rushing to my face.

As I opened my mouth to speak, my voice quivered. Ingrained in me was the little voice that said, *Women do not have a voice and children should be seen, not heard.* Surprisingly, in my second year of high school, I had to be told to hold any further questions in religion class so that the teacher, Miss Kennedy, could continue with her curriculum. (I send my belated apology to Miss Kennedy and I sympathize with all teachers who have to deal with difficult students.) I had initially asked a question because I was desperate to know the answer. My classmates seized the opportunity and used me to keep the teacher engaged on topics outside the curriculum. I have since determined that my need for acceptance by my classmates was stronger than my fear of speaking up. **Our actions are always motivated by a need or desire, regardless of whether it is worthwhile.**

Scholastically Not So Bright

At the end of each school term, I was always amazed that I wasn't at the bottom of the class. In a class of thirty I placed in the mid-twenties. For me, school was confusing. I understood the importance of Math and English, and the idea of communicating in another language, Spanish, interested me. English Literature was fascinating, although I never quite got the hang of *olde* English. Miss Bygrave, our English Literature teacher, was absolutely in love with the subject and she demonstrated great poise. She occasionally interspersed little life nuggets during her classes. I hear Miss Bygrave's caution in my head to this day to never leave home without making my bed. Teachers have a unique opportunity to pass on values to their students and it is an opportunity that is not taken advantage of as much as it should be. One Christmas, I was fortunate to have my name picked by her for the exchange of gifts. Her gift of an apple and a pair of stockings with a note that said "an apple to grow on and stockings to wear when you do" was memorable because it made me feel important. **How you make someone feel is more important than what you give them.** I believe that was the birth of my inclination always to wear stockings when dressed.

Geography was somewhat interesting, but I could not fathom why I had to remember dates in History. I had gathered that school was a necessity to attain a piece of paper so I could get a job at the end, and all I had to do was get passing grades. I had somehow deduced that it was not necessary to excel, or it was my excuse to not expect too much of myself.

I was selected along with a few of my classmates to sit the very first Jamaica School Certificate examination instead of the General Certificate of Education examination. I guess we were the guinea pigs, and it may have been because we were not as smart as the other children. We all passed, and even though it was a recognized educational certificate, I felt cheated. **Recognition only has a value if the person recognized puts a value on it.** This process had set me back one year because it meant I would have to wait until the following year to sit the general certificate test for the "O" (ordinary) level.

When I took Biology, I flunked the subject because I hated to be around cut-up dead animals and the smell of formaldehyde. Often I sat at the very back of the lab to avoid looking at the animal. I passed what I deemed to be the important subjects—Spanish, English, Math—and that was sufficient as far as I was concerned. I watched some of my brighter classmates with awe as they moved on to sixth form (the most senior level in high school), and proceeded to sit their "A" (advanced) level exam. I am willing to bet that at least one of them, Myrtle Hoo Ping Kong, has gone on to be a surgeon. She was always top of the class and won several prizes, and she was our valedictorian. She just seemed to do everything so perfectly and yet she was not boastful. Despite knowing that there were others who were smarter than I was, I still felt a sense of accomplishment. In the fog of confusion, I had still managed to graduate from high school. **Take pride in even small accomplishments.**

Another of my high school classmates was Jeannie. She had been my regular playmate after school in the lower grades as we would circle the humongous tree right outside the school assembly hall. It delayed my going home, as home had become an unpleasant place to be. The circumference of its trunk may well have been twenty-five feet, and the roots had huge nodes, sometimes the size of a baby's head. We challenged each other to jump from root to root without touching the ground. Jeannie was another smart girl who went on to sit her A level exams and I wish I knew where she is, because I believe she loaned me a small sum of money and I would love to repay her, although I cannot repay her friendship that was so important to me then. **You can't put a price on friendship**.

On my last day of high school, a number of nuns asked when they were going to see me. I thought they meant my visiting them but soon realized they had expected that I would to join the convent. I had at one time aspired to be a nun. By the same token I had also wanted to be a flight attendant—from one end of the spectrum to the other. Those aspirations, however, had long since left me, and my goal at the time was simply to acquire the skills I needed to get a job.

Puppy Love

I first noticed I liked boys back in elementary school at about the age of ten. Dexter was shy but very cute. I don't think he was the least bit interested in me, but I liked him nonetheless. Andre was a tiny guy who was impish, and I knew he liked me, because he said so, and I liked him because he liked me but I preferred his older brother Wayne. Both Andre and Wayne Matthews had been neighbors when I was a wee little girl, and their older sister Maureen had been friends with my sister Vi. There were other "nice looking" boys that took my fancy but I never shared my feelings with anyone. I considered it improper to speak about those thoughts.

When Mama rented one of her properties nearby to the Chin Sangs, their youngest son Easton was cute, and I fantasized that he and I were in a relationship. He was perhaps five or six years older than I. I was only twelve. He always visited us and chummed around with my brother Donald. Mama had no reason to think he posed a threat. Little did she know that Easton was secretly attempting to seduce me. Whenever he came close behind me, ran his hand under my neck, and placed his lips right by my ear, it sent shivers throughout my body. It went no further but it left me yearning for something more, although at the time I was not sure what that "more" was.

It was fortunate perhaps that I later learned that he had been visiting a nearby orphanage to see a girl or girls. It may have been innocent but immediately I painted him with the same brush as that for my father and he no longer interested me, although I still liked him as a friend.

In the Catholic all-girls high school I attended, the standards were very strict. Our dress code required us to wear navy blue tunics and short-sleeve white blouses with white crochet belts. Our school badge and house pins were worn on the left shoulder of the tunic. Our navy blue beret had to be worn at all times except during classes and recesses. We also wore brown socks and brown loafers. On P.E. (Phys Ed) days, we wore white blouses and box-pleated white skirts, white tennis shoes, and white socks. The white skirt had buttons all down the front so we could easily remove our skirts to reveal our long white bloomers for exercise. Again, the beret, school badge, and house pins were part of the dress. Makeup and jewelry were not allowed, and the length of the uniforms had to be halfway between the knees and the feet. Tardiness was met with detention and lines, and absenteeism was not tolerated. If you were seen anywhere speaking to a boy in your uniform you were also punished with detention after school.

Consequently, we girls resorted to walking two bus stops further than we had to, just so we could be at the corner of South Camp Road and North Street, because we knew that the high school boys from St. George's College and Kingston College would also walk from their schools past several stops to be at the same bus stop where we were. We exchanged glances with the boys and tittered among ourselves. After letting a couple of buses go by, we would hop on our bus and be satisfied.

I fantasized about one boy, Bruce James, who probably did not even know I existed. I probably even made a fool of myself by sending a message to him through one of my classmates, Andrea Chen See, who knew him, and my message was never acknowledged.

That was okay, because as soon as another boy tickled my fancy, I forgot about the previous one. Young girls and boys tend to be pretty fickle, and perhaps for a good reason, because in no way are they ready for any kind of relationship at that age.

My first boyfriend, Ernest, was a tall, gangly, skinny guy who had a winning smile and a love of photography. In my opinion, the photo he captured of me looking at a rose could have been a prize-winning photo. Of course, he also captured my heart with the words on the back of it: "Love thou the rose yet leave it on the stem." It didn't matter that he had taken photos of my cousin June, as well as a neighbor, Janet. On June's (or maybe it was Janet's) photo, he had written "It looked as if butter would not melt in her mouth."

Ernest usually rode his bicycle to my home. We went to Mass together and saw a few movies together. We just liked being together, but for the most part we were with the rest of the neighborhood kids, going swimming, to parties, or to the movies. I can't recall that we even kissed, but we considered ourselves boyfriend and girlfriend. So it was with a heavy heart that I bade him goodbye at the airport when he left for England to study to become an engineer. I cried openly, and his little brother Frankie put his arms around me and consoled me, saying, "He'll be back." Following Ernest's departure, his mom invited me to her home, where she tried to tell me I was still young and there was no reason to be so heartbroken. **Sometimes it is difficult for teenagers to see the wisdom in the words of their elders, and elders cannot understand why young people will not heed their sage advice.** I kept in touch with her for many years because in some ways it made me feel more connected to Ernest.

The letters between Ernest and me went back and forth for a while. They did not help to take away the sadness, and eventually he wrote one day to say I should not wait for him. I surmised that he had met someone else. I was disappointed, but in a strange way it was also a relief because it just didn't feel complete having a long distance relationship. **If you feel something is missing, there probably is.**

Women Want to Believe in Fairy Tales

Women have been sold a bill of goods that a Prince Charming will rescue us, marry us, and we will live happily ever after. Even in the face of alarming statistics that almost 50 percent of marriages end in divorce, women still long for the fairy tale to come true. I was no different, despite having grown up with a father who did not pull his weight and who was abusive. My family history also set me up to dread what I expected would happen when I grew up. Additionally, it set me up to rebel against a loveless marriage and to desperately long for someone to be what I imagined to be the model husband.

I had led a sheltered life and did not know much about relationships. Thus, when Ray, the guy next door, broke his arm, and he mistook my empathy for affection, and he began to send me romantic cards, letters, and flowers, I was swept off my feet. I'm sure many a sixteen-year-old gal would have reacted in the same way. **Until we have acquired true self-knowledge and realize we cannot look for happiness outside of ourselves, we inevitably make decisions based upon faulty information.**

It was convenient. He was the boy next door and so there was not much Mama could do about preventing us from seeing each other. It was obvious Ray was head over heels in love with me, and he showered me with the attention I craved. It was therefore no surprise that I reciprocated. **When you're young and someone tells you he loves you, you feel compelled to say you love him too and not take responsibility for your own feelings.**

I needed affection regardless of the source, and so when Ray proposed to me two years later, marrying him just seemed like the thing to do. When we broke the news to his parents, they were ecstatic, and his dad opened up a bottle of champagne to celebrate.

On the other hand, when we broke the news to Mama, she could not hide her disappointment. Neighbors and relatives encouraged Mama to block the marriage because they felt he was not good for me. For some reason Mama felt helpless to do so. I have only recently learned that my brother Sterling had discouraged Mama from blocking the marriage.

He had apparently suggested to Mama that I was emotionally fragile and could conceivably kill myself if she tried to block the marriage. How ludicrous! I would never have considered such a thing, but perhaps upon seeing my apparently love-struck state, Sterling did not know what to expect.

On one occasion when Ray got into a fight with his physically disabled brother, Freddy, Mama called out from her window to Ray to stop fighting with his brother. Ray's response was "Mind your own f-----g business." I was absolutely appalled that he would speak to Mama in that manner and I told Mama I was not going to marry him. To my surprise, she said, "It's too late, you've given your word and you must keep it." It could have been that her value of honoring one's word was so huge to her that she could not condone my going back on my promise. The other reason could have been that she wanted to avoid embarrassment. Regardless, I did not follow my gut feeling, and I proceeded with the plans for the wedding. **Your gut is there to protect you—listen to it.**

Ray's family was reputed to be very dysfunctional, perhaps in a slightly different way than ours. His father was the provider; however, he was a man of ill temper. He was reputed to have caused the physical handicap of his son, Freddy. How much of this is true is unclear. I first heard the rumor from a person who knew of the family when I was in Miami, Florida, shopping for my wedding gown. She warned me not to marry Ray. I had also heard from someone who worked in the polio clinic where Freddy attended that his condition was not polio related as the family wanted everyone to believe.

All that I knew about marriages and families was from books. I had read books where the man and woman got married, had children, and lived happily ever after in a house with a white picket fence.

When we got married I was barely nineteen, naïve and very unworldly. Our first home was a small rental apartment in a not-so-ideal part of town. It wasn't my picture of the perfect world, and I was nervous to be there. We had rented the apartment in a hurry because it had been two weeks before the wedding when I asked Ray where we were going to live, and he had not even thought about it. Then again, neither had I. In retrospect, it is clear that neither of us was really ready for marriage.

We later found a semi-detached rental home on the grounds of an estate property. It was a big improvement, but our landlord was an old Chinese man who seemed to lead a very complicated life. He introduced me to a lady who I thought was his wife, then another woman came on the scene and the first lady moved out. Later, another younger woman arrived, and both women continued living with him in the main house. It became apparent that the women were not related and that both were vying for his affection. His bathroom window availed him no privacy from our living room, and he could be seen at night having a shower with one or another of his "wives."

Nonetheless the semi-detached bungalow seemed like home, and except for the occasional scream next-door from our neighbor Gretchen, it was pretty peaceful. Gretchen and I both hated lizards and chameleons, which invariably invited themselves into our home. Whenever I heard her scream, I was secretly thankful the lizard or the chameleon was in her home and not mine. I was terrified of them when they entered our home, and instead of screaming, I quickly reached for the Baygon spray to kill them. I hated nothing more than to look up above my head while in bed and see a chameleon poised to jump.

When I married, Sterling was the only child left at home with Mama and Papa. Sterling was already thirty years old, and Mama said the house was too big for them. Mama determined that they would sell the house and move into one of the units in her triplex apartment building. Violet had moved to New York some years earlier. Donald had gone to England on a government grant that would allow him to be trained as a mechanical engineer with the proviso he had to return to Jamaica and work for the government for at least five years. Sterling went off and rented a place with a friend of his, and Mama and Papa were without a place to stay because the house sold before Mama was able to get a vacant unit in her triplex.

Ray and I took them in because we had two bedrooms. Mama and Papa stayed with us for about two months. Sterling visited us one day after not having kept in touch for a while. He told Mama about a townhome he wanted to purchase so that he could move in shortly after his upcoming marriage to Maria. There was a slight problem—he had no money for a down payment. His lifestyle of a new car each year and an extensive wardrobe had not prepared him to purchase a home. Mama loaned him five thousand Jamaican dollars (at the time this was equivalent to ten thousand Canadian dollars) for the down payment, and she turned to me and suggested I should get a townhome as well. I told her I had no money for a down payment. After all, I had only been working a few years. Mama finally talked me into accepting her offer to loan me the money. It was too good an opportunity to pass up, particularly when I was able to get a mortgage from my employer, British-American Insurance Company, at a very good rate.

Our home was right beside Sterling's, and although the home did not have a white picket fence, we had a white ranch-type fence. Ray worked out of town and left on Monday mornings and returned every Friday evening. Left to my own devices, I played badminton twice a week, visited Mama and my few friends, and read.

Two years after our wedding day, I gave birth to my first son, Steve. The babies were kept in the nursery, row upon row, and only brought to the moms for feeding. In the hospital early the morning after, the nurse brought the baby in to me and laid him on the bed. The lights were not on, and I went to the washroom. When I returned and picked the baby up, I thought to myself, *He looks different, somewhat darker.* I dismissed the notion, and just the thought of having my baby in my arms evoked such a motherly love—it was indescribable. Imagine my dismay when the nurse came rushing in very soon afterward to tell me that she had given me the wrong baby. It made me realize that **biological connection was not necessary for motherly love to exist.**

The night that I came home from the hospital, I sat in our living room. Soft music was playing and my baby, Steve (who had been returned to me), was fast asleep in his crib. I had the feeling that life couldn't be better. Ray and I both had decent jobs. He was a timekeeper with a construction company and I was working as a secretary at an insurance company. We owned our home, we had a car, and we had a beautiful baby. *This* was what I had read about in books!

I could not tell whether Steve had been getting enough breast milk. My breasts would swell painfully from being so full of milk. I was flying blind when it came to being a mother, except for the quick instructions I was given at the hospital. Mama had offered to come and stay with me but I foolishly turned her down just because I wanted to do it myself. **Don't be so proud that you refuse the help you really need.** Once I dispensed with breast feeding, I enjoyed being a new mom. I spent my days taking care of Steve, watching with wonder as he became aware of movements and sounds. He loved the crib mobile with the animals, and laughed and kicked, causing the mobile to move, which would make him laugh and kick some more. He was a beautiful baby. My heart filled with love, and I never left his side when he was awake. When he slept, I sterilized his feeding bottles, and I washed the numerous loads of laundry, which included baby clothes and cloth diapers. When I hung the clothes and diapers on the line in our backyard to dry in the tropical sun, I kept an ear open for any sounds signaling that Steve was awake. I even loved being a housewife as I prepared meals for Ray, whose work now was in Kingston, allowing him to come home each night. I looked through cookbooks and tried new recipes daily. Six weeks of maternity leave flew by quickly, and I wasn't sure whether I wanted to be at home with my baby or back at work. Both appealed to me.

Mama had offered to care for Steve and so did my mother-in-law. Fortunately, they lived not a great distance from my office and within walking distance of each other, and they took turns caring for Steve.

I had returned to work only a short time when I discovered I was pregnant once more. Feeling light-headed when I hung the diapers out to dry was not from lack of sleep after all. "Oh no," I exclaimed. This prompted my gynecologist to ask how strongly I felt about this. I told him that I was disappointed at the timing but since I had intended to have two children anyway, I was not going to play God and decide which child would be allowed to be born. Thankfully, I was spared the misery of morning sickness and the typical maladies many women suffer during pregnancy.

On the evening of October 22, Ray and I sat at the dinner table eating, when the first contraction took me by surprise. Five minutes later there was another. Ray went down the road to a neighbor who had a phone to call the doctor. The message was "get her to the hospital fast." Stubbornly, I refused to go until I had finished my dinner. The memory of being so hungry after Steve was born was too vivid in my mind, and I was not going to have a repeat of that feeling. Within half an hour of our arrival at the hospital, Christopher made his entrance into the world. Mama and Papa and my mother-in-law and father-in-law were all at the hospital. My father-in-law, when he was shown Christopher, said to him, "Your father is now working just to pay hospital bills and feed the whole family." His comment was insulting, because my employer's insurance plan had covered my entire hospital bill, and I was earning just as much as Ray and contributing fully to the household.

Mama and Papa took the bus to the hospital and brought chicken-and-wine soup for me every day, as they did when Steve was born, to bring me back to health. I don't think Mama realized that the wine was not a good idea since I was attempting to breast feed. Neither did I, for that matter. Women did not talk openly about breast feeding and information was not as accessible as it is today.

Chris was a colicky baby. He woke every night crying. I fed him, thinking he was hungry, causing him to throw up on my nightgown, on the floor, and sometimes on the wall if I was standing close enough to it. Eventually he would settle down, allowing me to clean up the mess. Ray would sleep through the entire ordeal. After several nights of no sleep, I eventually found the solution—a pacifier. Whenever it fell out of the crib, Chris awoke, crying. At least I knew that once I had cleaned it off in boiling hot water and let it cool and returned it to his mouth, he was content. Another solution to ensure undisturbed sleep was using a diaper pin and a short ribbon to attach the pacifier to his clothing. Eventually Chris would feel around in his crib, find it, and put it back in his mouth. As a toddler he called his pacifier "dut dut."

Steve was eleven months old when Chris was born and commenced being competitive for my attention. Steve let it be known that he too wanted attention.

After six weeks of maternity leave, I returned to work. I had only just then figured out how to juggle taking care of two children.

We hired a live-in nanny who we thought would be excellent. She was matronly and I consequently thought she was able to take care of the two tots. One evening I found the key to the liquor cabinet on the mat in our bedroom. I thought it was strange and went to examine the liquor cabinet. Ray and I did not drink but had some alcohol on hand in case we had guests who did. The bottles were emptier than I recalled having left them. I began to be suspicious and marked the labels lightly with a pencil. The next day the levels in some bottles were higher than the mark (she had added water to the bottles) and others were lower. When I accosted the nanny and drained the alcohol in the sink, she tried to discourage me from doing so. It was like throwing away water in front of a person parched with thirst in the desert. I fired her. Afterward, I was told by a neighbor that she had often heard my babies crying all day. My heart ached to think of how my children had suffered while I went out to earn an income. **Children are precious gifts and need to be given priority in our lives.**

I later engaged a new nanny who was younger. She was a good cook. Curiously, however, the meats I purchased seemed to be used up quickly. One day I decided to return home without notice to just check on things, only to cross paths with her boyfriend who was just leaving with packages. The mystery of the quickly disappearing meats was solved. She too was fired, and I was fortunate to find a day care facility whose owner was a former nurse. That gave me so much peace of mind; what I paid for it was worth every penny and more. Also, it prepared me for the North American lifestyle I would adopt a couple of years later.

I was too engrossed in the responsibility as a parent to thoroughly enjoy my children. The memories of real enjoyment are few, although I remember as if it were yesterday Steve taking his very first steps as he walked across the bed we had fashioned into a huge crib for him. Not long after that he took to wearing my clunky high heels as he enjoyed the sound they made on the terrazzo tile floors. It still touches my heart as I recall little two-year-old Chris bringing me a weed he had picked and put into his little toy milk bottle, handing it to me, saying "This is for you, Mom." The Little Red Caboose story was their bedtime favorite, and shortly after the three of us ended the story—"and the little red caboose always came last"—we cuddled together to fall asleep. After half an hour, I crawled into my own bed, exhausted from a day at work, fixing dinner, washing dishes, and taking care of the children. Given the chance to go back, I would spend more time enjoying my kids, creating more fond memories, rather than focusing on the weight of my responsibility as I did. I can't turn back the hands of time and all I can do now is to maintain a close and loving relationship with them and with their children.

Reality Sinks In

As the years went by, I began to feel so horribly lonely. I was not being fed emotionally, physically, or spiritually—I was empty. On Friday evenings and on Saturday and Sunday, Ray played poker with his friends, one of whom happened to be my brother Donald, and I was left caring for the two children, cooking and ironing. I even made sure that Ray and the other guys got lunch and dinner. My childhood belief that *I have to make others happy to be appreciated* was in action again. Apart from work and the children, I had no other outlet, and I had not cultivated or maintained my friendships. I felt imprisoned and everything was a chore, a responsibility. Was I reliving Mama's life—sacrificing myself, accepting responsibility for everyone, and being a slave to duty?

I questioned myself whether I was wrong to think such thoughts. The flowers and the cards had stopped, the romance ended, Ray was displaying signs of a bad temperament, and his tendency to use physical discipline on the children appeared. I began to wonder if the stories about his father were true and whether this ill temper was in the genes. I became increasingly unhappy, yet I did not vocalize my unhappiness. In my idealism, I expected that he ought to know I was unhappy and that surely he must know what his role as a husband and father ought to be. You likely know the proverbial saying: "When you assume, you make an 'a**' of 'u' and 'me.'" I was young, naïve, and unschooled in the art of communication. **Men are not clairvoyant, and unless women**

convey their feelings and thoughts we can't expect them to know what we are thinking or how we feel.

Instead of communicating with Ray, I had countless conversations with myself inside my head, as if somehow by osmosis Ray would get it. On the few occasions when we took the children to the beach or for a drive, I spent the time reflecting on how miserable I was, instead of being in the moment to enjoy the outing. It wasn't only that I did not know how to communicate; I also was burdened by memories from my childhood. Because of my childhood experiences, I had become super sensitive to anyone speaking to me any louder than in a normal tone of voice. The vitriolic and loud sound of my father's voice had made an indelible imprint on my mind. Another factor was the memory of my fright as a young child of four, when I had witnessed the loud and physical fighting of two workmen doing renovations on Mama's shop at 6 Victoria Street. A pick axe had been used to draw blood from one of the men, and the sick feeling in my stomach that I felt then would reappear whenever Ray used his harsh tone. Also, the memory of the hookers brawling outside of the bar across from Mama's 20 Gold Street shop triggered a sick, helpless feeling inside of me, and so any indication of discord between Ray and me drove me to withdraw and refrain from even commenting on everyday occurrences in case he did not agree. Ray was perhaps not even aware this was how I processed the conversation, and I guess at the time neither did I. I was simply reacting based on my conditioning, and he was just being who he was. **Communication is vital to a healthy relationship, yet we have not been schooled in this art.**

Work and Other Influences

My first job was as a steno-typist. The company was located in an industrial area quite some distance from home, and I had to travel an hour and a half and change buses twice in order to get to work.

One of the bosses who was already picking up another staff member offered to transport me to and from work. This was great, until that boss started to make advances toward me.

I did not know how to handle this situation. On the one hand I knew what he was attempting to do was morally wrong (plus, I was not attracted to him). On the other hand, I knew I depended on him to get to work. Fortunately, I was able to resist his advances diplomatically, and I resolved to find myself another job. In the meantime, the unwanted attention continued. At work, the access to the washroom was via the lunchroom. Consequently, whenever I knew he was in the lunchroom alone, I avoided going to the washroom. If I made a mistake, he grabbed at me as I went by. Sexual harassment in the workplace was not spoken of back then, and likely I would have been the one let go if I had complained. To his credit, he loaned me his vehicle to go to my interview for another job.

The next five years was a huge learning experience. I not only worked in a lovely modern office, but also I worked for a man named Peter Phillips, who taught me the finer art of letter writing and how to make others feel important. He had a system of recording important dates for each staff member, and he took time out from his busy schedule to see and chat with that employee for a few minutes to recognize that day, whether a birthday, employment anniversary, or wedding anniversary. It was not perfunctory; he was genuinely interested in them and spent a few minutes with the employee chatting about the employee's family or hobby or work. He looked people in the eye and he genuinely listened. He had a twinkle in his eye and a great sense of humor. Everyone loved him.

I followed Peter in his promotions all the way up to his position as vice president, and I was always challenged to take on new responsibilities. Along with my promotions came increases in pay, which made me feel appreciated and worthwhile.

I appreciated perks like free uniforms, discounted food in the lovely cafeteria on the fifth floor where we had hot lunches for less than a dollar. The cafeteria was one of my favorite places. On my very first day, I had gone up to lunch and sat timidly at a table on my own. Up came Yvonne Linton with her tray, smiling and welcoming me to the firm. She sat down, assuring me that I did not have to sit on my own.

One never knows what a simple gesture as an act of kindness can lead to. Yvonne is now my lifelong friend.

The auditorium on the same floor as the cafeteria had plush carpets and dark blue auditorium-style seats. This was the venue for staff meetings and special functions, such as the monthly women's hour, the organizing of which I was responsible, and the children's Christmas party. As the personnel administrator, I was challenged to speak in front of staff gatherings, and the more I did so, the more comfortable I became with speaking to groups. **Challenge yourself to grow despite your discomfort. You will begin to wonder why you were ever afraid.**

The company placed a high priority on employee relationships, and a staff member from each department was selected to sit on the entertainment committee. Employees were well compensated, their job responsibilities were clearly set out, and performance was recognized. Employees were made to feel important and they were given the opportunity to participate in important decisions.

Eventually, Peter was transferred, and after that it wasn't quite the same for me, and so after five years with British-American, I went looking for greener pastures. I joined a reputable travel agency and tour operator—Martins Jamaica Limited. There, I had the opportunity of traveling, and the job challenged me to grow. I had to overcome my shyness. My job entailed negotiating with hoteliers and tour providers and transportation companies at various destinations for package rates. I also dealt with advertising agencies and airlines and made in-person presentations to businesses on behalf of the travel agency. Initially I was hesitant to take on a job that entailed speaking with others, but I accepted the challenge and found it was not such a big ordeal after all. People were just people. **Accepting the opportunity to get out of your comfort zone encourages growth.**

As I became more aware of the larger world and what it offered, the more depressing my situation at home seemed. I longed for more. I was learning so much from my work and I was maturing socially. The gap between Ray and me grew even wider, and I was so ignorant about what I could have done to rejuvenate our marriage. My childhood programming included a lot of Roman Catholic indoctrination and I knew it was wrong to be unfaithful, even in thought. It did not stop my yearning, and these feelings created such dissonance within me that I believe my constant migraines were simply a manifestation of that discord.

A Change in Scenery

Jamaica was experiencing political unrest and an economic downturn. The class struggle reared its ugly head in the form of threats and physical attacks against non-blacks, and I, like many others, began to feel unsafe. This was when Mama decided to leave Jamaica for Hong Kong. Fear was rampant, and I began to be extremely nervous. One evening, I was waiting at a traffic light when someone walked alongside the vehicle. A sense of panic overcame me and I felt as if my heart had jumped right into my mouth. On another evening, as I pulled into our carport, I saw a man walking up the road in my direction. I hastily jumped out of my vehicle and fumbled frantically to find my key for the gate to our wrought iron fencing that enclosed our porch for safety. Perhaps the man lived in the neighborhood and was simply out for a walk, yet I did not want to take a chance, as he might have been there to harm me. One night, after we heard gun shots in the park by our house and someone running right by my bedroom window, it became abundantly clear that we could not continue to live in fear. Ray and I, perhaps mostly I, decided to migrate to Canada. I was hoping that moving to a new country might solve our relationship problems. I didn't recognize at the time that **wherever you go there you are–different place/same person.**

We sold our home and moved to a rental home close by to my in-laws, since our departure date was not to be for another two weeks. It was a nice home, but I soon learned that the carpet hid countless small cockroaches, and I felt dirty sleeping there. In preparation for our move, we purchased furniture to ship to Toronto, Canada, and busied ourselves with building crates to protect the furniture during its transit to Toronto in August 1976. As a precaution, I sprayed everything that we packed to ensure that no roaches would accompany us to our new home.

No one was allowed to take more than five hundred Jamaican dollars (the then equivalent of one thousand Canadian dollars) out of the country. The country of Jamaica was not in a very good economic situation and there were many who secreted money out of the country, taking the risk of being caught and jailed. A coworker offered her services, stating she knew someone who would safely transport our money to Toronto for us. I was reluctant but Ray suggested that we take her up on the offer, since there seemed to be no other way. We lost everything we gave her. We never saw a penny of it again. This was a huge blow, because this "friend" was perhaps the first person to betray my trust. I could not believe it. I could not accept it, because it was not something I would have done. Once more I had failed to listen to my instincts and had regretted it. **Often individuals who may appear willing to help you are merely opportunists who take advantage of your vulnerability.**

We arrived in Canada and lived with Ray's brother for a couple of weeks until our rental apartment was ready. In the first week of our arrival, I said to Ray, "You need to go find a job first." He wasn't taking any steps, and after a week I decided one of us needed to start earning an income. Thankfully, I was able to get a job very quickly. I enrolled the children in a home day care to allow Ray to find a job. When I came home, Ray and the kids were there, but nothing had been done, and he made no effort to help with preparing or cooking supper. He made no efforts to do the laundry or to give the kids a bath and help them with their homework. I do not blame him entirely, because I could have advised him what my expectations were. **No one knows what we expect unless we tell them.** Unfortunately also, boys in Jamaica were raised to believe that they are not expected to do much, if anything, in the home. **We tend to be products of our upbringing unless we learn, grow, and take action to change who we are.**

Most importantly, Ray made no efforts to find a job. Instead, with what little resources we had, he went to Honest Ed's bargain store with his friend, who happened to be my very first boyfriend, Ernest.

They were both supposed to be looking for jobs. Ray came home with bargains that we didn't need and couldn't afford. This went on for a while and increasingly the situation became very burdensome and frustrating.

We had been in Canada for almost six months and he was still unemployed. We were paying rent, paying babysitters, and living on my salary as a secretary, which was not very much at the time. Then Ray's mother died and he flew to Jamaica for the funeral. We had some money left back in Jamaica. However, instead of thinking to bring some of it back for us to live on, he contributed all that we had left to his mother's funeral, although it was likely not needed. This was a source of huge contention between us. **Financial disagreement is one of the leading causes of marriage breakdowns.** It was almost a year before he was able to find a job with a Fotomat store where he was the maintenance man. His job was to clean the booths and do repairs and whatever else needed to be done. He was given a vehicle with the job.

He complained that he was not able to get a better paying job because he was not qualified. In an effort to be helpful, I encouraged him to go to school to get qualified. He did one semester at Centennial College and received excellent grades, but after that course he simply refused to continue his schooling. His excuse was that he had only gone because I told him to go. I became frustrated, because financially we were drowning.

Since he decided not to further his education, I told him I would because I instinctively knew that a post-secondary education would be required in order to command a better job and better pay. I applied to York University, in Toronto, and worked on a business administration undergraduate degree for five years part-time, on a program that would have required three years on a full-time basis. I had mapped out exactly what courses I had to do from day one and all the prerequisites. I had formulated in my mind what my end goal was and what I had to do to reach it. It meant not taking any holidays. It meant studying at every available opportunity and attending classes on two nights each week when school was in session. It meant sacrifice, because initially when I went to York we had no vehicle and I had to take two buses and a subway to get home from school. The bus services were not as efficient as they are today, and it took me over two hours to get home. Oftentimes, when I returned home after class at approximately 11:00 p.m., the children were still up. They hadn't had their baths and they hadn't done their homework. They usually at least had eaten dinner, as I had prepared the meals in advance so that all Ray had to do was reheat the food. Ray would be slouched in front of the TV watching the hockey game.

In 1981, I thought I was pregnant once more. Fortunately, I was not, but the fear of having another child with a person upon whom I could not depend, a person I did not love and a person who was abusive, made me decide to have my tubes tied. That too was a disappointment, because Ray dropped me off at the hospital and left me there. It had not occurred to me then how disappointed Ray would be at my decision. I could only focus on what I needed to do. I was to be operated on the next day and able to go home the day of the operation. There were complications. My blood pressure had dropped too rapidly and the surgeon had difficulty performing the laparoscopy. As a result, he had to make a big incision across my stomach, requiring me to stay hospitalized for a week. Ray did not phone, and he did not come to visit me, even though he was on strike at the time and could easily have visited. I had to phone to find out how the boys were doing. Mama had called the house, and after quite a few times of not reaching me at home, she was able to get the story from him that I was in the hospital. I had not told Mama previously about the operation because I did not want to worry her. She insisted that Ray take her to the hospital to see me. That was the only reason he came to the hospital. If I had any hesitation before of leaving the marriage, it was now gone. When I returned home, Mama was the one who came to take care of me. I could not depend on Ray to do that.

Around that same time, I had become friends with a fellow student at York University and confided in him about my marital situation. He apparently was not entirely happy with his marriage, and we commenced consoling each other and soothing our wounded egos. So many individuals make this horrible mistake which could lead to an extramarital affair. First of all, consider that starting an extramarital relationship not only hurts you (you are selling yourself short; you deserve a fully committed relationship) but it also hurts others who may not deserve to be hurt. Many people also jump too quickly from a failing or failed relationship into another relationship. If individuals were to direct as much effort into their marriages as they do into starting a new relationship, there might be less divorce. To focus on your own marriage, take time to reassess what has gone wrong, accept responsibility for your actions in contributing to the state of the relationship, make a mutual commitment or recommitment with your spouse, and make a concerted effort to notice the positive things about your spouse every day and learn to communicate in his or her love language. (See *The Five Love Languages* by Gary Chapman.) Not all marriages can be saved, especially if left unattended for too long or if there are addiction issues or physical violence, but **if individuals are fully committed to each other and to the marriage and they invest in that commitment daily and learn to communicate in each other's love language, they can have a marriage that they will cherish.** I did not have this kind of knowledge back then, and the deterioration of our marriage had occurred over several years. Furthermore, it does take two willing parties to make a marriage work.

Ray exposed the children to habits which were unacceptable to me. He freely grazed in the grocery stores, a habit I did not want my children to adopt. On one occasion, he bought a barbecue set, one of those cheap briquette types that you can take to the park. Upon arriving home he found there were three in the package instead of one. Instead of taking them back to the store, he returned to the store and purchased at least one or two more packages of the same type so that he could give them to his brother or others. That was not a value I was prepared to accept, and to me it was dishonest. I could perhaps have understood if he had simply recognized there was a mistake and not bothered to return the extra items. When he capitalized on the mistake it challenged the very value I cherished the most—honesty.

Another habit he engaged in was to bring home supplies that he found at his workplace, like paper towels and toilet paper. I was mortified, because it was not how I was brought up, nor what I believed in, and I did not want to teach dishonesty to my children. As kids, if we came home from school with a strange pencil, Mama sent us right back to school to return it.

I argued with Ray constantly about what was right or wrong, but that alone was not enough to convince me to end the marriage. He routinely physically disciplined the children and it became too much to bear. When Chris was merely four or five years old, Ray had left his camera on a tripod in the room. Chris, as any kid of his age would be tempted to do, went to look at the camera, knocking it over on the carpeted floor in the process. Ray took his belt and used it on Chris. Chris had been walking around with just his underwear, and the belt wrapped around his leg, making a cut on his leg that was dreadfully close to his testicles. I became very upset because I realized how dangerously close Ray was to doing irreparable harm to my son. We had words about it. In my heart I knew this shouldn't have happened and that it was wrong, but I still didn't know what to do about it.

I had seen signs previously of Ray's bad temper. When Steve was only three or four and had fallen asleep in the vehicle, he was still sleepy when the vehicle came to a stop. Steve did not want to get out. Ray screamed at him and yanked him out of the vehicle. I knew it was wrong, but I didn't know what to do about it. I made my displeasure known, but that was all I felt I could do. The last straw came when I was away at a seminar in California. I had been sent there by my company, Woods Gordon, at which I had been promoted as a research analyst. When I came home, Steve had a huge bruise on his chin. When I asked him what happened to his chin, I could tell he was avoiding my question. He had his eyes downcast and said, "I fell." His answer didn't ring true, so I asked Ray what had happened. His answer was, "I was mad, I had a coke bottle in my hand and I hit him with it." Coke bottles were large and made of glass, not plastic. I felt a wrenching in my heart. I was angry at him and disgusted that he was this type of person. In the pit of my stomach lurked a dread that Ray was exactly like his dad, that he was also like my dad, and that my poor children were helpless victims.

I went to work under this heavy cloud. I kept thinking about how unhappy I had been through the nine years of our marriage and how terrible it was that he was releasing whatever frustration he was feeling onto the children, and I cried. I was upset and could not concentrate. One of the principals I worked for asked me what was wrong. When I shared what had happened he said, "Rose, we're going to lunch and we're going to meet with my fiancé." I knew she was a social worker, but I had no idea at the time that she was under an obligation to let the Children's Aid Society know that my child had been a victim of abuse. When we spoke, she told me she had an obligation to report this incident and that the CAS would take my children from me, because they were at risk.

The thought of losing my children caused alarms to go off in my head and my heart. I pleaded with her not to let the authorities know. Her response was, "If you do not leave him, Rose, I will tell them." I asked for time. Thankfully, she agreed, even though it was probably against policy. At that point I knew I had no choice. I knew that it was too late for counseling because the children had suffered enough. They were exhibiting behaviors that had brought them to the vice principal's attention several times. The vice principal had once asked if I was a single mom. The children were soiling their pants and misbehaving, and when the child psychiatrist spoke to us after having seen the children for some time, he said, "Nothing is wrong with the children; it is you adults." He looked at Ray and me, and when we talked about our relationship, he told Ray he had his head buried in the sand. He also said I was at fault, because I had a responsibility to help my husband grow with me.

What did I know? I was a young girl when I got married. I had images of what a marriage should be and what an ideal husband should be. I had no clue that communication was important. I had all these thoughts in my head, but I had not been able to share them with Ray, because I thought that he should have known what it takes to be a good husband. We had tried marriage counseling, but Ray believed that I was the one totally at fault and denying it.

I felt that I had done everything a good wife should do, but I was not going to be able to change Ray and I was not prepared to accept him as he was. It is such a huge mistake to have expectations of your life partner to be a certain type of person when you know he is not now that kind of person. It is extremely important that you examine what your values are, what your expectations are, and spend the time to get to know your intended spouse before jumping into a marriage or a relationship. Without this knowledge, marriage may reveal some unwanted surprises. **Women marry men hoping they will change and men marry women hoping they won't.**

We had both been totally unprepared for marriage and we had allowed our marriage to deteriorate so badly; neither of us knew what to do. It was clear that Ray and I were too young and too immature when we first got married. We were not taught or shown by example what constitutes a good marriage, and we had blundered along the way, damaging each other's self-esteem and spirit.

In living with Ray, I was living with someone who did not share my values and who chose to physically discipline my children. It seemed I had no choice but to terminate our marriage or lose my children. It was a huge decision, because I was brought up to believe that you stayed married no matter what. Furthermore, being a Roman Catholic, you did not divorce—you stayed together, come hell or high water, and divorce was not an option.

Then, I thought of Mama. What would it do to her to think that her daughter was going to be divorced? What shame! My situation was nothing as bad as hers was. There were so many thoughts racing through my mind. I had been unhappy for nine years, and my programming held me back from thinking I could find a solution.

My religion also seemed to condemn me. I sought counseling through a priest, and when I recounted the events of our marriage and the abuse of the children, I was thankful for the words he spoke in our third session. He said to me, "Rose, do you think God is a forgiving God?" I said, "Yes." Then he said, "Rose, do you think God is a loving God?" I said, "Yes." Then he said to me, "Do you think God would want you to live this way?" And I said, "No." It lifted a huge burden from my shoulders. I thought to myself, at least I can now believe that God would not be angry at me for divorcing Ray. Mama had once questioned whether my life was so terrible because God was angry at me for not becoming a nun. Why is it that we tend to think of God as a condemning and angry God and forget that He is a loving God?

When I broke the news to Mama, she was actually relieved. In fact, she said I should never have married him. This was the same person who had told me I had no choice but to proceed with the marriage because I had made a promise. I never delved into the reason why she had changed her thinking. Perhaps she realized how unhappy I was and how terrible my situation was. How often have we done or not done things because we are afraid of what others may think of us? **We need to make sound decisions without concerning ourselves about what others think about us because what others think about us is none of our business.**

When the decision was made, we put our house up for sale. It was a lovely house, but realistically it was over our budget. We had a first, second, and third mortgage, and when Ray had been on strike, our financial situation became so desperate that I resorted to selling off pieces of jewelry that I had accumulated over the years to pay our mortgage. I did manage to hold on to a few pieces of jewelry that came from Mama because they had sentimental value and meaning. During the years that she was suffering from financial woes she had held on to them for us. Mama usually handed the necklaces and bracelets to my sister Vi and me just before we went to a wedding and when we came home, we had to hand them back. She carefully hid them behind a closet drawer so Papa was not able to get at them to sell them for gambling money. When my sister and I each got married, we were each given our gold cross chain and the gold coin bracelet she had saved for us. These remain our connection to our childhood. Mama had had financial difficulties and could have sold them but did not. So to me they mean a lot. I could not part with them, but I parted with so many other pieces in order to pay the bills. I had to do that twice, and I felt ashamed each time I had to enter that store.

It had not occurred to Ray to moonlight, although I, on the other hand, took whatever overtime was available. To work the extra hours on weekends, I had even brought the children with me and kept them occupied with paperclips, paper, pens, pencils, and stapler.

When Ray was asked by the realtor what we paid for our mortgage or taxes, he had no idea what these amounts were. His lack of knowledge also explained why he chose to do very little to increase our household income. I take responsibility for creating that scenario, because I controlled the money. Ray handed his paycheck to me each week and I gave him a small amount for spending money. Later, when I attempted to include him in the finances, he saw no reason to change things. **It is so important for couples to be both aware of the household finances and to work together toward a shared goal.**

I was disappointed that my marriage was ending, because it meant I had to admit failure. I was also relieved, however. We lived together in the house while it was up for sale, which was a strain. We carried on as if things were normal, but they were not.

I noticed Ray becoming depressed. I also noticed that he was angry, and my nurturing nature took over. I made a point of talking with him, trying to boost him up, reassuring him that it wasn't really his fault, that it was both our faults, that we were married so young and knowing so little and leaving things to go wrong for too long. One evening I awoke in the middle of the night and noticed he was not in bed. I went downstairs to find him sitting in the dark, and there was an envelope addressed to me on the coffee table. I picked it up and he immediately grabbed it from me. I presumed it to be a suicide note. It put fear into my heart and I spoke with him until I thought he was okay. I don't remember exactly what was said, but I decided at the time that I could not sleep knowing that I and my children could be at risk. From then on until we moved, I slept in my children's bedroom, because I was determined to protect them no matter what and would die protecting them, if necessary. It did not deter me from my decision to leave. I knew I had to for my own sanity and to protect my children. **The emotional fallout from the breakdown of a relationship can be**

extremely devastating, especially to the person who does not want the relationship to end.

I continued to talk with Ray throughout those last days together to assure him that he was a good person, and I even considered and probably wrongly told him that we could continue to be friends. I say wrongly because that is difficult, especially if one person still wants the relationship. Moving day came and he helped us move. The boys and I moved to a rental apartment. The very next day Ray came to the apartment asking to take us out for dinner. We did go out for dinner. We did try to maintain some semblance of normalcy for the children, but it became clear after a while that he was hoping to reconcile with me. I did not want to mislead him and I knew that once I had left, there was no turning back, because it had taken nine years for me to leave. **Separation takes its toll on both parties regardless of who makes the decision.**

The separation, however, was more difficult for Ray emotionally and mentally than for me. The process was easy to an extent, because Ray simply signed the separation agreement prepared for me by my lawyer. Ray and I divided monies and agreed on joint custody. We also agreed on access and child support. He was perfect in availing himself of access and appeared almost to have *changed* into an attentive father. The boys looked forward to seeing him, and things appeared to be fine. Unfortunately, I spoke ill of him to the children at times. This occurred on at least one occasion when he bought a hunting knife for Steve on one of their outings and I was appalled at his lack of judgment. Steve had been vocal about hating his brother Chris and I did not want any mishap to occur and so confiscated the knife from Steve. In doing so, my comments about his Dad's stupidity was not pretty. My reaction was perhaps understandable but in looking back, I realize I could have handled it differently. **Parents do not realize the negative effect that derogatory comments against the other parent can have on children.**

While Ray and I were separated, there were times that I found it hard being a single parent, especially one who worked a lot. The kids were getting somewhat out of hand having so much free time on their own. Between us, we decided that perhaps it was best for them to go live with Ray. He was beginning to show more interest in them and spend more time with them, and it appeared he had more patience with them than he had previously.

The first birthday that was celebrated after our separation was Chris's. I had invited Ray to join us for the sake of the children. When Steve's birthday came around, however, I decided not to invite Ray to the party. It seemed best, as I did not want to feed Ray's hopes of us reconciling. The boys were living with him at that time. When I returned the boys home to Ray after our celebration, I asked to have a word with him because there were some papers I needed him to sign for Christopher. As we spoke together, he asked me to move back to Jamaica with him. His request came out of the blue. I was surprised because it had been quite some time since we had separated, and he had never before approached the subject of reconciliation. Even if he had, I know my answer still would have been "no." I looked at him and said, "I'm sorry, I can't."

"I knew you would say that," he said. His breath was short and heavy, and there was hate burning in his eyes.

I watched him in disbelief as he sprang to move behind a couch, picked up a rifle, and loaded it. For some strange reason, it all seemed to be in slow motion.

I said to the boys, "Call the police."

Ray yanked the phone from the wall and said, "No one is calling the f---ing police."

"Go to your room and stay there," I commanded the boys.

I stood there, knees shaking and heart pounding. I kept talking to Ray, trying to tell him that it was not totally his fault that we were separated—that we grew apart and there were circumstances that would prevent us from ever being a couple again. I also told him that he was basically a good person and that he could move on and find someone else. Those may not have been the right words to use, because all he did was cock the rifle, and he aimed it at me while continuing to swear. I saw my life flash before me. It was as if I could actually hear my thoughts shouting "this is it." Although a part of me could not accept that this was the end of my life, I resigned myself to dying. I made the sign of the cross and started praying "Our Father, who art in heaven, hallowed be thy name …" The act of doing so must have had an effect on Ray because he emptied the shells on to the floor, threw the rifle down, and ran out.

With my whole body trembling, I walked trancelike to the boys' bedroom only to find the room empty. I stared unbelievingly toward the open window and my stomach churned as if I was about to hurl. I dreaded what I might see outside the window, but I just had to go to the window. I had to know. The apartment was on the third floor. Where had they gone? I looked outside and I could not see the boys. I was relieved to see an overhang at the entrance, which I later learned the boys had jumped onto to get to the ground. I made my way downstairs still zombie-like and as I got to the back of the building, my boys were there. We hugged each other and cried. We were shaken by the experience. The police cruisers drove up with lights flashing and the officers jumped out of the vehicle and spoke to me. There were three cruisers because a neighbor who had seen the boys jump out of the window had also called the police. Fortunately for us, Adam, a friend of the boys, had been with them, and he was a little more mature than my boys. I believe he was instrumental in getting them to jump out of the window and to call the police.

I led the police up the stairs to the third floor. It was like in the movies. They held their guns up against their chest, coming out tentatively from behind the wall after making sure it was safe to do so. When they got to the apartment they saw the rifle on the floor. They picked it up, searched the apartment, and then we left. They took me and Chris home. Steve had chosen to go to his friend's home. When I got home, the police took my report and left. At that time I was living with a gentleman named Ken who was much older than I was. Unfortunately, I knew my sons could not live with me, because Ken wanted nothing to do with kids. I did not know what to do. I was helpless. That night I called Ray's brother to let him know that the police were looking for Ray. Despite what he had done or could have done, I still felt a need to watch out for him. Ray later turned himself in and was charged.

Months later, when the matter came to court, I was subpoenaed as a witness. As suggested by Ray's lawyer, I wrote a letter in which I pleaded for the court to have leniency and not to incarcerate Ray. I could not see that it would have been beneficial for him or for the children, and I honestly felt that it was best for him to receive counseling. The judge made remarks suggesting that I had provoked the incident. I was livid. That was not what had happened. I got up and told the judge that I had been at Ray's home because of our children, that we had something to discuss about the children, and that I had not provoked the incident. The judge told Ray's counsel, "Shut that woman up or I will find her in contempt of court."

I was being treated as if I were the accused—not the victim. I had come close to death and it didn't seem to matter to the judge. At that very moment, I felt I had to do what I could to ensure no other woman would endure this humiliation. I wasn't too sure how I would do this but I knew it was wrong for a judge to further victimize a victim. I could have chosen to be vengeful toward Ray. I had every reason to hate him, and yet I did not. I felt sorry for him. I understood that his desperation might have driven him to do this. Truthfully, his actions were unacceptable, but I could not hate him, because he is the father of my children.

Ray got a suspended sentence. In the time that followed, he would continue to provide a home for our two sons until they grew older and moved out on their own.

Years later my children asked me, "Mom, what did you ever see in Dad?" My answer was "I was very young, but I don't regret it because now I have you."

It is important to understand that **no matter what you've suffered, no matter what you've been through, no matter what your choices were, they have brought you to where you are today. There is a reason why you're here at this particular point in your life. We learn from our pasts, and we learn what we need to do to change our futures.**

I fully recognize that I did not always make wise choices, but those choices are responsible for where I am today.

I allowed that one event to control my life for many years. I was not able to drive in Ray's neighborhood without looking over my shoulders, without fear of what he might do and how he might react if he saw me. My life became a secret and I was plagued by nightmares. My children were complicit in keeping my secret. It was a heavy burden on them. I recognize that now, but thankfully, they did it willingly without me asking them. Later on when I knew they had relaxed in their vigilance, I had to remind them not to divulge any information about me to their father. I was still afraid. I was afraid for a very, very long time. I made my prison from my own fear.

My nightmares are vivid. In them Ray is trying to harm me or my son Christopher. In my nightmares, I am shot or I narrowly escape. When I awaken, my heart is racing at an alarming rate. Even though I assure myself it was only a dream, I question whether the dream is really a warning. After all, I had had a warning in a dream before Ray pointed a loaded gun at me, and I have come to believe our dreams are there to help us. I lie awake, sometimes for hours, and my faith in God slowly resurfaces and I rely on Him to keep me safe and to keep Ray safe from wrongdoing. I believe Ray is now happy, and I really hope he is, because everyone deserves happiness. **Our actions in the past should not condemn us if we are truly repentant. None of us is blameless**.

When my son Chris was getting married some seven years ago, he asked me if I would be okay to be in the same room with his dad. Guessing what the occasion would be, I readily answered, "If it's important to you, I'm okay with it." It wasn't just because Chris was getting married, it was because I had taken part in a "Cleansing Stream" program with my church that allowed me to let go of all the past hurts I had experienced in my life. At that time I had forgiven and released anyone who had ever hurt me or anyone who I thought had hurt me. More importantly, I forgave myself for having ever hurt anyone. It was definitely cleansing. I learned also that forgiveness did not mean that what they did was okay.

I would be lying if I said I do not sometimes still feel uneasy or fearful. What happened was a traumatic, near-death experience, one that is imprinted deeply into my physiology. I do, however, remind myself when there is doubt that God spared me for a higher purpose and I must make this second chance worthwhile.

Trust Must Be Earned

I had thought I would never remarry, but I did marry Ken eventually. Our interactions would turn out to be an on-again, off-again relationship lasting about a decade. Ken was the man I had been living with. He was an older gentleman—twenty-five years older than I was—whose first wife had died of Lou Gehrig's disease. He had wooed me with lavish gifts, fine dining, and travel. After his first wife's death he had married his secretary, and later he had married a woman in the United States. I learned of this latter marriage only after our wedding. He had three adult children; there was one to whom he had not spoken in a very long time. Those were danger signs but I did not see them. I was simply too close to the situation. Our relationship was toxic. He was still chasing his second wife. He was seeing her and pretending he was not. There was always an excuse for why he had contacted her. I caught him in so many lies, and each time he was able to manipulate the truth and point the finger at me, stating that I was imagining things.

In the early part of our relationship we lived together for one year. During this time he convinced me to leave my job, and I took a pay cut of ten thousand dollars per year just to work with his private investigation company, which would allow me to travel with him whenever he wanted. I was at his beck and call twenty-four hours a day, at the office and at home. I was also almost always left hanging. Often I ate dinner alone because he had not come home for dinner when I had fully expected him to do so. I am embarrassed to say that there were several times he convinced me to take a cab to where he was so that I could drive him home from some bar because he had drunk too much. I found that the bargain I had struck was not worth the price I paid. **Your self-worth is the value you put on yourself, not what someone else determines your value to be.**

I was so upset with the lies and feeling unloved, taken for granted, and mentally abused that I sought out a psychiatrist. The psychiatrist failed to see that I was in a codependent relationship, that I was looking for something that Ken was not able to give me, and that Ken was literally a replica of my father, except for the gambling. While under the care of a psychiatrist, I was prescribed antidepressants. In a heated argument with Ken, I threatened to take them all. I put them into my mouth, but I immediately spat them out. It was my desperate cry for attention. I even found myself once threatening to jump off the seventeenth floor balcony and had one foot up on a planter. Whether I would have gone, I'm not sure. What I did know was that I was not getting what I needed and I was extremely unhappy.

Ken offered to come with me to the psychiatrist to help me. The psychiatrist always had dandruff on his jacket and invariably nodded off to sleep during the sessions. Ken's attendance proved to be just an attempt on his part to deflect any judgment away from him. He told the psychiatrist that I had attempted suicide. When I retreated to the psychiatrist's washroom, the psychiatrist panicked and called the police. In the washroom he had a coffee maker and a coffee pot, a cheese board, and a knife. Suicide, however, was far from my mind. I was too upset at Ken's deception—he pretended to care and led me to believe he wanted to help.

When the police arrived, they wanted to escort me to the North York Hospital. Ken asked to take me there himself, and although they agreed, they followed him. When I was seen by the psychiatrist on duty, he was puzzled as to why I was there. I told him I wondered why myself. Ken frequently said during the later years, "I should have let them institutionalize you." No doubt I had given up too much of my control to an undeserving fiend and to an unprofessional psychiatrist. **Not all psychiatrists are competent. Do not give them more power than they deserve.**

Sometimes we tend to learn lessons the hard way. This was certainly one of them, because I did not know why I chose to be with this man. I had first been attracted to Ken by his charm. I was also carried away with the travel benefits, entertainment, and the lure of a good life. I soon learned that giving away a piece of me was too high a price to pay. I gave away my self-worth and I lost my identity. He needed to be the center of attention, and he gained that by belittling me, criticizing me, or making fun of me. Eleanor Roosevelt once said that **no one can make you feel inferior without your consent.** I had given him consent to make me feel inferior and I had taught him how to mistreat me.

The relationship had driven me to distraction. I no longer felt competent. I no longer felt in charge of my life. I was so depressed that I indeed might have been suicidal. I really don't know whether I was or whether I used the threat to get the attention that I wanted. We separated one year after we had been living together, but I continued working with Ken. He lived in his own place and I lived in mine; this was difficult because I wanted desperately to be with him. Yet I knew that he was not a person of integrity. He was not truthful. **It is crucial that your partner in life share your values.**

For some reason, because of whatever unmet needs that I had, we finally reconciled. I moved into Ken's apartment and we lived together. Things were fine for another year (at least I thought they were) and we got married. He had not been speaking with his son, Roger, for some time, and it did not feel right to me that Roger would not be at our wedding. I decided to call Ken's daughter Mary in British Columbia to see if she could intervene and convince Roger to come to the wedding. Mary was excited and said she would have Roger, who lived in Pickering, Ontario, attend the wedding. She also asked excitedly, "Can I come also?" then just as quickly said, "Oh Rose, do you know what you're doing?" That should have clued me in, but I was oblivious to the danger signs. I said "of course" and made arrangements to fly her in. The wedding was marvelous, and only my close friends Phyllis, Yvonne, Joanne, and Jennifer and my children and Roger and Mary knew in advance that we were getting married. The other guests believed they were attending a Christmas party. In effect, we had a surprise wedding. It was a beautiful wedding, all planned in a matter of three weeks.

After about six months into our marriage, we had moved into our condo. We were traveling, and we had a summer home. By all accounts we should have been happy, but it didn't last. The lies resurfaced. Ken's cell phone bills were enormous—over four hundred dollars per month. I decided to look into it, and it became obvious that he had been having lengthy conversations with a woman who worked at an insurance company. Whenever I questioned him about it, he got defensive. It came to a head, and I was beside myself because I had centered my whole life on this man.

I went to a psychotherapist who told me that I should not believe that my husband is having an affair unless I find him naked in bed with someone else. This psychotherapist was in fact condoning Ken's behavior and devaluing my feelings. A health professional is not God. **Trust your instincts**. I was totally out of control and I became desperate. I longed to be loved. I longed to be valued, but I was not. Our relationship deteriorated to where we were constantly arguing, and Ken threatened to hit me. On a couple of occasions, he rough handled me and boasted that as an ex-cop he knew how to ensure there were no telltale bruises. I was often upset and I cried a lot. I spoke to my sister on the phone and confided in her, until Ken came and pulled the phone away from me to try to give his version of the story. He proceeded to tell my sister that I was "mental," that I was crazy, and my sister, bless her soul, defended me. In that conversation, he picked up the phone, motioning to throw it at me. I realized I could not live with a deranged person. There were so many arguments that I felt desperate and frightened. In the middle of arguments, I fled the home and went for walks or drives because I just had to get away. My actions reminded me of Mama when she went for long bus rides just to escape from her reality. I also realized how deep a depression I was experiencing when I found myself walking in the rain in the middle of a thunderstorm when normally I would be so scared of lightning. I did not care. I desperately needed to escape.

Acknowledging that I needed to do something for myself instead of being a slave to someone who did not appreciate me, I decided to apply for law school. My visits to a law office with Mama when I was a young girl, my attendance at court for Ray's assault charge, and my Small Claims Court agency work had led me to believe I could make a positive difference as a lawyer. I researched and planned what I had to do to get there. I knew I had to take the Law School Admission Test and so decided to take a preparation course and bought LSAT sample tests. I did everything I could to ensure my success. Unfortunately, the night before I sat for my LSAT, Ken and I had a huge argument that affected my test performance the next day. The mental abuse and belittling continued.

On Christmas Eve 1991, he left for Vancouver to see his daughter without even advising me beforehand. I had just returned from St. Kitts, where I had gone for refuge from the madness, on the recommendation of my hypnotherapist. I had taken all my LSAT papers and my applications to the various Law Schools with me to work on while I was there. I had called home each day, only to be told that I was a silly girl, that I was stupid, and that there wasn't anyone else. Yet, when I returned, I noticed the Christmas presents were moved to the dining table away from the tree, and certain things were out of place—things that Ken would not touch normally. Then I learned he had entertained a woman in our home, as well as her daughter, her sister, and others. I told him that was inappropriate, and I knew something was amiss when he told me he had taken our comforter to the dry cleaners. At least he had the decency to have it cleaned!

We argued into the night, and he left for his Vancouver trip without me. I was miserable, emotionally and physically. I had a horrible migraine with nausea. Nonetheless, I carried on and had my kids with me for Christmas. On Christmas morning, Ken called to tell me it was my fault that he was on his own for the holiday. It turned out that his daughter Sue had told him they had been invited to dinner and she hoped he wouldn't mind. He had assumed that he was also invited, but that was not the case. So, not taking any responsibility for his own actions, he blamed me. It was the worst Christmas I ever had. I was extremely unhappy, and my only consolation was that I was with my children. For years after, I hated Christmas because it reminded me of that horrible experience.

While Ken was away, I got a telephone call advising me of his affair with the woman whom he had entertained in our home and who was even younger than I was. When he returned and I accosted him about it, he denied it. We continued to argue. The arguments got out of control, whereby I felt I was going crazy—that I was actually crazy this time like he'd been telling me for years. I finally had had enough. I packed what I could into my vehicle. I called a friend, Jackie, and asked if I could live with her, and she agreed. I had no idea where I was going to get any money or how I was going to live, except I had some credit cards. I had a little money in the bank, but not very much. Everything I had was invested into that condo and our life together. Ken was mad that I left. He continued to try to charm me back and to get me to continue working for him. I did work with him for a little while, difficult as that was, but only because I had no other means of supporting myself. I did what I had to do, but I did not like it.

Desperation is a horrible thing and can cause you to lose your rationality. Driving back to my girlfriend's home one day, I passed a house sporting a sign—"Psychic Reading"—and automatically my car turned into the driveway. I must have had "Sucker" written across my forehead. The lady told me there was a way to win my husband back, and gave me explicit instructions to go to a high-end men's clothing store on Bloor Street in Toronto to pick out a specific jacket, size "large," and bring it to her. The jacket cost over two hundred dollars, money I really did not have, but I was willing to do anything. She also gave me water that was treated with some magic potion to put into his drink. So, whenever I went to the condo, I would secretly put the potion (which was quite likely plain water) into his jug. I had placed my future into the hands of someone else—a shyster, no less. I am sure those who know me now will not believe I could have been so stupid, and although I hate to admit it, I acted stupidly.

On the other hand, desperation can spur you on to find a solution. I knew I was unhappy with the person I had become. I had given up my control and I was no longer the self-assured person I used to be. I knew I needed help to regain my self-esteem and I realized that I was not in a place to do it alone. A course advertised in the *Toronto Star*, offering help to individuals who wanted to increase their self-esteem, was the answer to my quiet prayer for help. The course was excellent, and it helped me on my road to recovery.

Perhaps it was fortuitous that I was successful in getting into law school before the "potion" ever worked on Ken! I nervously opened the envelope, and upon reading the acceptance letter, I punched my fist into the air and exclaimed "Yes!" This was the very first time I showed any excitement about anything. What a great feeling. Previously, as a result of listening to Mama, who taught me to be humble, I had always contained my excitement no matter what. **Learn to celebrate your successes—both big and small**.

Not only was I accepted at Osgoode Hall Law School, but also I was accepted at UVIC in Victoria, British Columbia, and wait listed for Queens in Kingston, Ontario. It was difficult to envision living away from my children and so I gave up on the idea of moving to British Columbia.

I made arrangements and got an apartment on the York University campus, near Osgoode Hall Law School. For three and a half years my home was a small one-room bed-sitter. I walked across the street to school each day.

Although the law school told us not to work while doing this program, I knew I had to do something else to support myself. I obtained a part-time job in the legal department of a finance company, which was happy to accommodate my schedule, and for a small stipend I performed work in an office at school. That, along with a student loan, helped me to make my dream possible.

Law school was grueling, because I had been away from mainstream education for about ten years. Also, the other students were so young— young enough to be my own children. As it turned out, however, I blended in and was just like one of them. They had dinner parties to which I was invited, and I in turn invited them. It could have been that I was the only one with the appliances and kitchen tools they needed!

In the meantime, Ken had refused to pay me for anything from my part of the investment in the condo as well as for my years of having worked with him for less than what I had before, and my lost opportunities. His position was that he would rather pay all the money to a lawyer than let me have anything. He alleged that when he met me I had nothing but a pot to pee in. This was so demeaning to me when I considered what I had given up. I had reduced my income by ten thousand dollars per year, plus I had foregone whatever increases I would have made. In relying on his promise of a happy life together, I gave up my dignity and I also gave up my self-esteem. I had invested into the condo the money that I had from my inheritance from Mama, along with other money I had managed to save. I also paid the condo fees and all other household expenses when we were together (except the cost of our trips). I even paid the condo fees for six months after I left, because that obligation was paid by post-dated checks from my account and I had not changed that. In fact, when my post-dated checks ran out and Ken was billed for the condo fees, he expressed amazement at how much we had been paying. It was a hard decision, but I decided, for the sake of my sanity and my studies, that I needed him out of my life—money or no money. I told him he could keep his stinking money, that I did not need it, and that I could do this on my own. I think he was surprised, but telling him that was the most freeing thing I ever did.

Anything worth having has a price.
Ask yourself if you are willing to pay the price.

After my second year of law school, Ken again contacted me. He needed me to help him with his business. I told him it would have to be a purely business arrangement where I would work for him that summer for a set sum, no strings attached. He agreed, but that did not stop him from trying to charm me. While in his office, I got confirmation that his lover had, in fact, been his lover for at least a year after we were married. She indicated that she had the impression that I was in an insane asylum because of how he spoke about me. Too many women are quick to buy into sob stories of "My wife doesn't understand me." **Men often tell lies that women are prepared to accept.**

I enrolled in all kinds of personal development courses. I spent a ton of money because I knew I needed to do something to pull myself out of this hole that I had dug, the one I had allowed him to drag me into. It took years and years of reading motivational and inspirational books and taking courses, but I slowly regained my self-esteem and assertiveness.

When I graduated from law school, Ken managed to charm his way back into my life. I had a celebration party for my graduation and he was invited. At the party, it became so obvious that he had not changed. He was now seeing someone else (the daughter of an old friend of his) and his lover from before had become the one who was being cheated against. He had told his current lover where he was and was summoned by phone at the restaurant to take her call during my celebration. It was insult enough that this occurred, but he drew attention to himself by announcing "my public wants me." He was a megalomaniac, something I had not acknowledged before. After that evening, I told him that I never wanted to see him again, and he went out of my life for a while.

Me and my substitute Mom, Jo Baker at my Call to the Bar

I did my internship as a student-at-law in personal injury litigation, and upon obtaining my license to practice law, I jumped in with both feet and hung out my shingle. I opened up my own general practice firm, taking criminal and family law cases as well as real estate work.

I bumped into Ken at court one day and he deceived me into thinking he had realized how fortunate he was to have had me in his life. Prior to that occasion he had never said he was sorry, yet here he was saying what a fool he was. I foolishly thought, *He's getting older; maybe he's come to his senses.* We resumed our relationship.

We had been reconciled only a year when I started to notice the telltale signs again. He began having secret phone calls. He went to Cuba several times a year, and I found love letters to him written in Spanish. He could not read them, but I could. I realized there was more to his trips than what he tried to make me believe—that he was a Good

Samaritan, simply taking down clothing and linen for the natives in Cuba. He did this under the guise of being a good guy, when in reality he was just feeding his vice of wanting more and more women. That was totally unacceptable to me, and so we argued and we fought.

In early 2000, we parted company for the last time. By then, I had incurred huge debts, since I had fallen back into the same trap of paying for everything while we were together, securing nothing for me. I walked away with a loss so huge that it has taken me several years to recover. But I left with my sanity once more and a stronger resolve to be responsible for myself and to never give up what my true essence is to anyone or for anyone.

We need to value who we are at our deepest level and never give this up to anyone or for anyone.

On the day before my birthday in 2000, Ken walked into my office with a dozen red roses to wish me a happy birthday. He also told me that I was going to be served with divorce papers the next day. I told him to get out of my office and to take the roses with him. As always, Ken wanted to look like the nice guy, and as he went out of my office, he told my secretary that I was not happy, as if I should be!

I felt an urgent need to get away from Toronto, as if by leaving the area, I could shake the dust off and have a "do-over." I managed to find a position in a law firm in Barrie, in southern Ontario, and decided to close up my practice in Toronto. My girlfriend Nicole offered to have me stay in her Horseshoe Valley home for a reduced rent, and it was too attractive not to accept.

After only six months of being with the firm, I learned that they were disbanding the partnership and that family law was not going to be part of their remaining practice. My supervising lawyer, Tessa, and I were given the opportunity of renting space from them, but that would mean going back into private practice. I was not yet ready to do so, particularly when I had just given up a very busy practice in Toronto. I had just purchased my own home in Barrie, and the idea of giving that up was also not very appealing. It was my very first home on my own and I found gardening very refreshing. I considered going back to

Toronto to live, since there were more work opportunities there. The deciding factor was that I had found a church in Barrie which was so warm and welcoming that I was reluctant to let that go. My experience at Mapleview Community Church reawakened the deep relationship I felt I had with God in my youthful days and it was exactly what I needed.

Luckily, I joined another small law firm and we had a very mutually rewarding working relationship for over four years. I was finally making very good money, I liked the people in the firm, and I enjoyed what I was doing. The only drawback was the commute back and forth each day. Nonetheless, without any significant other in my life, I was able to make it work, and with a little adjustment in my hours, it was ideal. Eventually the commute took its toll, however. I found myself nodding off to sleep while on the 401 Highway or ending up in Mississauga after a long day at work because I had missed the 400 exit. I suppose it didn't help that I was experiencing menopause at the time and was becoming quite forgetful.

I did have a couple of romantic liaisons, and because I was in a position of strength, not neediness, I was able to discern when the relationships were not contributing anything to my life. One relationship I had was quite pleasurable, since Mo was a die-hard romantic. When I entered his apartment, invariably I was met with soft lights, music, and flowers in the room specially bought for the occasion. On a couple of occasions he had even rose petals on the bed. I was under no illusion that we would ever progress beyond romance, and I enjoyed the relationship for what it was. After a couple of years of just dating, however, I realized there was no real substance to our interactions, and with a sad heart I broke off the relationship. **Relationships need to be about more than romance.** For the first time in my life, I had taken the driver's seat. Thankfully, Mo saw that what we had was more than just a romantic relationship—we had a great friendship and we were able to continue being friends without a physical relationship. I did not realize how much I cared for him until he died of cancer some years later. I attended his funeral service and it suddenly hit me that I did care deeply for him, and shedding tears for him gave me the closure I needed.

I also discarded another relationship in a matter of months, when I realized that this person was insecure and insanely jealous. I could not smile at anyone or speak to anyone and I was criticized for wearing my skirts too short or for "always looking at men." We were in a restaurant one day when I looked toward the back of the restaurant where a dad and his two sons were interacting. I found the scene quite charming. All my companion saw when he looked to where I had been looking, however, was the man, and he accused me of flirting with the man. He had no future outlook on life, became unemployed, and was also very needy. Furthermore, he was much younger than I and wanted to have a family. For a very fleeting, crazy moment I had contemplated adopting a child. This was before I really knew him. Crazy, huh? I assessed the situation and decided I did not need someone who was like a child that I had to take care of. Furthermore, it was no fun being around someone who always wore a scowl on his face. **It's better to be alone than to be in a bad relationship.**

Great care should be taken in selecting a mate, and romance is not enough, although it helps. There needs to be depth to a relationship. In addition, your mate should be someone who trusts you and shares your values. Although you don't need to share every interest, having a common interest is very important.

I regret the decisions I made in the past in the area of relationships. I also regret the financial decisions I made in the past. I am sure many of you have. The pity parties I held for myself grew tiresome and they were not fun. I grew tired of using my childhood story as an excuse for my lack of success in love and finances. I took courage in remembering that Mama had been through worse yet had survived. I knew that some part of me was like her and that I would survive. I just had to do whatever I could to make myself better. Many years went by before I could let go of the past, let go of any kind of resentment or hard feelings that I had against Ken or about any of my other relationships.

It was some time before I reached what I call a state of emotional neutrality. I neither hated Ken nor loved or pitied him. I recognized that he lost out by our parting, because I had been prepared to love him despite our age difference (he was twenty-five years my senior) and to take care of him despite any health problems that might befall him. However, he chose his path and, as a result, I chose mine.

In 2002, I consciously decided that my life was fine the way it was, and I was prepared to live my life on my own. I had a house (well, the bank owned part of it), I had a very well paying job, I had my sons (who were not living with me but were very much a part of my life), I had my friends, and most importantly I had my health. My life was together.

Many will say that when you're not looking for love, it will find you. Perhaps that is true. Carole (a friend I had worked with) and I walked into the Alladin Banquet Hall to a singles dance. As we paid our entrance fee, I looked up and saw a man. I would later find out his name was Ted. I thought to myself, *He's different.* I had told Carole earlier that she should go in with a mindset of just having a good time and not expecting to meet Mr. Right, since "You'll find that it's a bunch of losers who go to places like this." Carole was nursing a broken heart and wanted to go out for fun. Since I love dancing, I had suggested the Alladin.

Like vultures after a kill, men swarmed to us as soon as we sat down. Ted was not among them. Although somewhat disappointed, I reminded myself that I was there to dance, and I did.

When I finally took a break and sat for more than five minutes, Ted came over and asked me to dance. He remarked that I had been a busy girl. I replied that I like dancing, not that I really knew how to dance. He chuckled and said, "You seemed to have been doing fine out there." His words told me he had been noticing me, and I was pleased. After a couple of dances, he took me back to my seat and asked me to save him a dance for later. I said, "Sure." After a few dances more I wanted to say no to the others who came to ask me to dance but was afraid that if I did, Ted might be scared to ask me to dance again. I went to the washroom and when I returned he quickly made his way to the table.

We danced for a while and unfortunately I had to leave. I was having an early start the next day to lead a training walk for the first 60 km Princess Margaret Hospital Breast Cancer Walk. Ted remarked that he had an early morning planned as well, as he had to go to work. He walked me to my car and kissed me on the cheek and said, "Perhaps I will see you again here in a couple of weeks." In the vehicle I turned to Carole and said, "We're coming back in two weeks." I had decided I liked him and wanted to see him again. How's that for a woman who was happy with her life the way it was?

Two weeks later, Carole and I walked in again to the Alladin and there Ted was, sitting in the same spot close to the bar. Carole and I had already decided we were not going to sit at a table but rather would stay close to the bar. I walked toward the bar and smiled at him as I went by and got my soda water with lime. Glass in hand, I went over to chat with him. After he invited me to sit beside him, we continued to engage in small talk until he asked me to dance. We were on the dance floor when he shared that he was kicking himself for not having gotten my number the last time. I boldly told him that if I could have, I would have kicked him also. He shared that he had told his daughter that he was coming there that night and she had told him to make sure he got my number this time. As we took a break from dancing, I did something so out of character that I surprised myself. I took out my business card, wrote my home number on it along with my personal e-mail, and asked him for his number and his e-mail. I had been so accustomed to having guys ask me for my number, and Ted had not done so. For some reason everything about Ted was different and nice.

We danced the rest of the night and he said he was glad I came in when I did, because he was just about to leave when he hadn't seen me there. He asked if I was interested in going for a walk, since he knew I enjoyed walking, and we made arrangements to go walking on one of the trails in Collingwood the following Sunday.

The next day Ted e-mailed me and said he was glad we met again and that he was looking forward to our walk the following week. Later that day, he called me from his cousin's baseball game to say it was too bad the following Sunday was so far away. Again, contrary to my usual cautious self, I said, "If you aren't busy on Saturday, why don't you come over for a barbeque?" Here I was—inviting a stranger to my home. What was I thinking? Where was that careful Rose who had chastised her friend Jackie several years prior for going to a stranger's home for a first meeting? For some reason, I knew I could trust Ted.

The week dragged, and finally Saturday arrived. I wanted the evening to be perfect. Ted showed up at my door, dressed casually in Bermuda shorts, a long sleeved sweater, and sandals, carrying a bottle of wine. We chatted endlessly as the conversation flowed so effortlessly. I knew only one way to cook steaks and that was well done. He graciously ate without complaint, and as far as I could tell the evening was a success. He said goodbye eventually at 11:00 p.m., bending to give me a kiss on the cheek. I had such a good feeling about that man. He was a gentleman. Our second date was the very next day.

I arrived in Collingwood at the walking trail and changed into athletic shoes, and we hit the trail, continuing our conversation where we had left off the night before. After walking for close to an hour, we decided to go for dinner. Following dinner, we went for a walk down by the grain elevators in Collingwood. The temperature was perfect and it seemed as if God was smiling down at us. We parted company, promising to keep in touch.

That Thanksgiving I met Ted's longtime friend of over fifty years, his children, his mother, and his siblings and their families. He also met my children, my friends, and my family.

As time passed, we grew to know each other very well. Although over the three years we dated he sometimes spoke of "when we live together," I managed to avoid the topic. I wanted to be absolutely sure we were compatible, shared the same values, and had the same idea about relationships. I came to the conclusion that Ted was a very decent fellow. His friends and family loved him, and it was apparent he was well respected. Our kids got along famously together, and even though none of them lived with either of us, it was important for us that our kids approved of the relationship and got along well with each other. As I considered all of this, I initially hesitated, because Ted is not romantic, and I sometimes wondered whether he really loved me. It was only after reading *The Five Love Languages* by Gary Chapman that I began to understand that we each show love in different ways.

After Ted made several comments that suggested that we might live together, I finally told him this was not going to happen. I told him I believed in marriage, and as much as I loved him, if either one of us was not 200 percent certain that this would be for keeps, then I would prefer we simply remained friends rather than live together. He had assumed that since many of my friends were not married and just lived together, I would have wanted the same, although of course he thought we would eventually marry. I told him that while my friends may have been fine with living with someone, I knew that I was not prepared to live with him unless we were married. Living with him without marriage would have led me to believe—rightly or wrongly—that he thought I was not good enough for him to marry me. I had consciously decided that I never again wanted to feel that I am not enough. Marriage was not high on my priority list, since I had everything I needed and I had decided before I met Ted that I was content. **Women need to be sure of what they really want and not compromise just to please another person**.

The more we spoke about getting married, the more appealing the idea sounded. We spoke frankly about a premarital contract, what we expected would happen if, God forbid, we were to separate or one died before the other. It was no surprise that we took only fifteen minutes of discussing this to find out we were exactly on the same page. Ted and I are so similar in so many ways, it is almost spooky.

Me and Ted on our wedding day

Ted and I got married on June 10, 2006. I realize that the success of our relationship now is partially due to my failed relationships and the lessons I learned from them. It is perhaps more a result of my growth, learning about who I am, what my true essence is, what my values are, where I am, and where I want to be. I look at life differently now. I understand that I am in charge and that it's about making the right decisions and moving on. **Grow—not crumble—from your disappointments, learn who you are and what your true essence is, what your values are, and what you want out of life. Only then can you truly know what and who you want to be in your life.**

Like Helen Keller said, *"Face your problems and acknowledge them, but do not let them master you."*

I may not be responsible for being knocked down, but I am responsible for getting back up. It's not what happened to me that counts, it's what I did about it.

As Nelson Mandela said, *"When individuals rise above their circumstances and use problems to push them to become more, they grasp greatness."*

I may not have greatness right now, but I know it's within my reach if it's what I want.

I do not want revenge on my "ex," because if I seek revenge, I may as well dig two holes, one for me and one for him. I'm not prepared to do that. In looking back on my life and my mistakes, I understand that mistakes are not fatal. They have taught me valuable lessons.

Life can throw us curves. We tend to learn our greatest lessons from our most difficult relationships. For me, my most difficult relationship was with Ken, and it taught me I needed to value myself and not look to someone else to give me value. When I learned that lesson, I became stronger and more self-assured and confident that I was living an authentic life. It also propelled me to seek answers and it led me to find the mentors I mentioned before. I am on a journey of learning and growing to be a better person and a teacher to others.

We cannot blame our past or make excuses for our failures. We've been conditioned, and we've been told different things, but if we hang on to those crutches we will never move forward.

I could never have imagined it possible to be exactly where I am today. I look back at the challenges that I encountered in my life and realize that each of them were gifts given to me to grow and become a better person. I now mostly accept challenges that present themselves to me as an opportunity to grow and become a better person. I find that when faced with a challenge, I need to remind myself to "W.H.A.M." my challenge with the following process of thinking and action:

What's the problem?
How do I feel about this situation?
Accept or reject it?
Move my feet (take action).

Using this process, the challenge transforms itself into a gift, even though initially I may not have considered it a blessing.

Challenges can test us, but I promise that if you approach them rationally, you will eventually see they are indeed gifts.

Summary

- Love yourself, do not depend on others to love you.
- Hold true to your values, do not compromise your value for acceptance.
- Associate with people who will motivate and inspire you to become better individuals.
- Take responsibility for your own actions.
- There is no substitute for a good friend. Every woman should have at least one.
- Do not let other people's opinion of you determine your worth.
- It is not what happens to you that is important; it is how you deal with what happens to you.
- When you want a desired outcome, determine how you are going to accomplish it, do what is necessary to get it and pay the price to get it.
- The best way to stop feeling sorry for yourself is to give to others.
- How you make someone feel is more important than what you give them.
- Take pride in even small accomplishments.
- Do not look for happiness outside of yourself, take responsibility for your own feelings.
- Trust your instincts.
- Men are not clairvoyant, ask for what you need and share how you feel.
- Challenge yourself to grow despite your discomfort.
- Couples who are fully committed to each other and to the marriage and who invest in that commitment daily and learn to communicate in each other's love language can have a marriage they will cherish.
- No matter what you've suffered, no matter what you've been through, no matter what your choices were, they have brought you to where you are today. There is a reason why you're here

at this particular point in your life. We learn from our pasts, and we learn what we need to do to change our futures.

- Rise above your circumstances and use your problems to push you to become more and grasp greatness.
- It is better to be alone than to be in a bad relationship.
- Use the WHAM formula:
    - What's the problem?
    - How do I feel?
    - (Is it) Acceptable or changeable?
    - Move my feet to make changes.

Chapter 6

A Feeling of Discontentment

Time for a Change

MANY WILL VIEW MY STORY so far as a success. Despite the disadvantages of coming from a dysfunctional family, having no support in my early school studies, being ridiculed by my schoolmates, two failed marriages, being downsized, facing down the barrel of a loaded rifle, having to put myself through university and law school, and other challenges, I am a successful small-town family law attorney with a very good reputation and I am now happily married and have great personal relationships with friends and family.

I hasten to add that I have heard more-compelling stories of others who have faced what seemed like insurmountable challenges and were able to overcome them and become better individuals for those challenges. They are indeed a breed apart from others who have not had the privilege of facing challenges. I merely use my mother's story and mine—because I know them well—to illustrate that we do not have to be victims: we can unwrap the gifts hidden in those challenges and be better individuals for it.

As I have done throughout my adolescent and adult years, I am constantly reevaluating, and I currently recognize a feeling of discontentment. That familiar feeling of discontentment signals a need for change. I am still not where I want to be. I am not looking at this from a financial viewpoint. Recently I asked myself honestly whether I was living my purpose, and I do not have a satisfactory answer.

It was only some seven years earlier on New Year's Eve, the time of year when I tend to be introspective, that I actually wrote out what I believed was my purpose in life. "I am living my life to make a positive difference in the lives of others." It became a part of my e-mail signature and remains there today.

I had not previously clarified for myself what I meant by "making a positive difference." I understand now that what I really want is to help individuals deal with their life challenges in a very practical manner. I want to assist them to use those gifts sent in the disguise of challenges as stepping stones to improve all areas of their lives, including identifying, pursuing, and accomplishing their goals.

As a family law attorney I accomplish my life purpose to a certain extent, but more and more I realize that I am not reaching as many people as I could, and that as a lawyer it is difficult to become as personal as I would need to be to help my clients grow from their divorce or separation. I have also come to realize that the legal system is broken. No offense to many of the very wise and competent family judges we have in Simcoe County in Ontario, but there are some who are so removed from reality that more and more I am coming to the conclusion that families are not being served by the justice system. Individuals are spending large sums for legal fees, only to come away feeling that they were not heard or that nothing is happening fast enough. Invariably, the dominant personality litigants manage somehow to find litigious lawyers, who appear to have no regard for fairness or what really is in the best interests of the children or who feel the rules of the court do not apply to that lawyer. Unscrupulous lawyers are taking advantage of the parties' vulnerability and are not being held accountable by judges or the organized bar.

Lawyers are perhaps the only ones who benefit by the legal fees being charged for litigation. On the other hand, it is difficult for lawyers to provide service to clients who are slow in paying their fees. Many of us may have come into the profession with altruistic ideas, but when it comes down to reality, if the lawyer isn't paid he or she cannot survive. It is after all, a business.

I see the damage that is being done to individuals—most particularly to children—by vengeful spouses and acrimonious battles over money, and the fallout is that we are going to end up with children who become dysfunctional adults. Then, only God can help our society.

Regrettably, this system is broken, and I am not proud to be a part of a broken system. I want to help make this world a better place, so I will focus on assisting individuals who have already reached a decision to separate by using what is called the "collaborative process." This is a more respectful and less harmful process of resolving family issues. I recommend strongly that you read *A Tug of War* by Justice Harvey Brownstone, a Canadian judge, to learn how litigation does not serve the family. In addition, I will be doing what I can to educate the following: young adults, on how to choose and be the right partner; married couples, on how to keep the love alive in their marriages; divorced/separated individuals, on how to recover and grow from the experience; and individuals, particularly women, on how to be the best person they can be. My belief is that if we as individuals become whole as persons in our own right, our relationships cannot help but be healthy and there will be fewer breakdowns of relationships and marriages. It may be a pipe dream, but it is a task I am willing to undertake.

At the end of my days, I know what I want to be said about me, and I have now chosen to live my life accordingly.

I know this puts me in the spotlight and that I have bared my soul to all and sundry. However, I own up to my mistakes and take responsibility for them. I forgive everyone who has ever hurt me or who I imagined has hurt me, and I hope that anyone whom I have hurt will also forgive me. As human beings, we are not perfect, and it is quite likely that I will offend others as well as be offended by them. I ask that they accept in advance that it is not my intention to hurt or be hurt, and I hope that our interaction, no matter how brief, will leave us both better off.

Life Is Not Static

Have you noticed that life is not static? Circumstances change. People change. It has been said that there are only two things you can depend on in life—death and taxes. There really is a third thing: change. Even in nature, change is noticeable. You will notice that in dry seasons, the branches of trees may not grow as much, but their roots will go deeper in search of water. The more deeply rooted the tree is, the better chance it will survive and thrive. If a tree is crowded by other trees, it grows taller to find the sunlight.

Change is inevitable. As changes occur, we need to find ways to survive and thrive through those changes. We are not trees or plants; we are humans with the God given gifts of free will and intellect. We are in charge of our lives and we must make our decisions wisely each step of the way.

Summary

- Change is inevitable. Find ways to survive and thrive through changes.
- You are in charge of your life, you must make wise decisions each step of the way.
- A feeling of discontentment may signal a need for change.

Chapter 7

So What? Now What? Your New Story

What Defines You?

YOUR NAME, YOUR PROFESSION, YOUR financial standing, your color, and your creed do not define who you are. Your role in the family, such as wife, mother, or daughter, does not define you either. "What does?" you ask.

Who you are is defined by your true essence—who you are at your inner core, irrespective of anyone else or anything else. To know yourself, you need to ask, what is my essence? Who am I uniquely, at the deepest level within myself? Am I an honest person? Am I a caring person? Am I respectful of others and their property? Do I love others? Am I charitable in my words and deeds? Am I industrious? Am I ambitious or driven? These are just some of the questions we can ask ourselves. Of course there are varying degrees of some qualities, such as ambition, for example, but for others there are not—you are either honest or you are not. When you get the answers to your questions, you will have identified your authentic, genuine self.

Very few people, if any, ask themselves "Who am I?" That question requires introspection, which can be quite scary. What if I don't like what I see? Worse yet, what if I don't like what I see and I don't know how to fix it?

Who Defines You?

Too many of us blame who we are on our past and our childhood, where we received 95 percent of our internal programming.

In every conceivable manner the family is the link to our past, bridge to our future.

Alex Haley

What kind of conditioning did you receive in childhood? Was it negative? Were you told you were stupid? Maybe this was not said in a mean manner. Perhaps your mom or dad said, "Don't be stupid," or "Why are you always doing stupid things?" You may also have heard comments that made you feel you were not good enough or that you were an exasperating child. You may have been compared by well-meaning parents to some other kid who was smart, who got a scholarship, or who was so obedient. The problem is that words can have so much power. If you heard these remarks often enough you may have internalized them and thought of yourself as stupid, not good enough, frustrating, or "lesser than." Do these negative remarks really help you? Not usually, although in some cases they may cause you to try harder just to prove them to be wrong. In reality, it's not what you were told, it's what you interpreted those words to mean. Having been programmed, you may find yourself using those words to yourself even today. You may do something that is a mistake or an exercise of bad judgment and instead of saying, "Oh, I just made a mistake," or "I could have done ————," you say to yourself, "I'm so stupid," or "I'm such an idiot." Or you say, "I always ..."

One seemingly harmless remark is "I'll try." As the *Star Wars* character Yoda said, ***"Do ... or do not. There is no try."*** By saying "try" we set ourselves up for failure. Many times we continue the negative influence that we received as a child or a young adult. For instance, we may trip, and instead of recognizing it could happen to anyone we say, "I'm such a klutz. I'm good for nothing." We may also have learned to give up control and not be assertive as children and even as adults. Have you ever caught yourself in your relationship saying, "I don't care, it's up to you," instead of stating what you really would like to do, when asked?

On the other hand, you might have heard positive comments when you were young: "You're so smart"; "You're so talented"; "You're so pretty"; "You're so good natured"; "You're always so helpful"; "You're so obedient"; "You're such a good girl." Did you buy into it? Did you believe it? Usually these comments were meant to praise you. You could, on the other hand, have interpreted that you always have to be obedient, no matter what. Can you see how this could be unhelpful to you if you were in a controlling relationship? Can you also see that being helpful and being praised for being constantly helpful may sabotage you by leading you to believe you should always put yourself last? Being told you are good natured need not mean you have to take everything with a smile and not try to change an unacceptable situation. In a similar way, assessing "talent" is subjective. Everyone has talent. Everyone is good at something, no matter how unimportant it may be to someone else.

What happened to you as a child or young adult boils down to how you—yes, *you*—have interpreted it. In fact, a good life lesson to keep in mind is that "it's not what happens to you that matters, it's what you do with it."

The question you really should be asking yourself is, Am I being true to who I really am? Remember, we're considering your inner core. Are you being who you really are at your inner core, or instead who somebody else wants you to be? You need to be a first-rate version of yourself, not a second-rate version of someone else. Remember, you are one of a kind and you need to love who you are, because you are a child of God.

Our deepest fear is not that we are inadequate Our deepest fear is that we are powerful beyond measure. It is our light, not our darkness, that most frightens us. We ask ourselves, Who am I to be brilliant, gorgeous, talented, fabulous? Actually, who are you not to be? You are a child of God. Your playing small doesn't serve the world. There's nothing enlightened about shrinking so that other people won't feel insecure around you. We are all meant to shine, as children do. We were born to make manifest the glory of God that is within us. It's not just in some of us; it's in everyone. As we let our own light shine, we unconsciously give other people permission to do the same. As we're liberated from our own fear, our presence automatically liberates others.

Marianne Williamson

Were we treated differently because we were the oldest, the youngest, or the middle child? Were we treated differently because we were a boy or a girl? Sometimes our childhood gives us the tools to be that wonderful person we were meant to be. Sometimes it gives us conditioning that does not help or serve us. We need to remember that regardless of what we were conditioned to be or what we were told we were in personality or other characteristics, we are each one of a kind.

You are one of a kind.
There has never been and never again will be a human being like you.
There is nothing ordinary about you.
If you feel ordinary it is because you have chosen to hide the extraordinary parts of yourself from the world.
Today rejoice in your uniqueness
and share the gift of who you are with those around you.

Barbara DeAngelis

Breaking the Cycle

You've read Mama's story, you've read my story. I am sure you have also read or heard other stories of individuals who refused to be defined by their humble or dysfunctional upbringings or by their seemingly dire circumstances in life and have gone on to make a significant difference. I'd like to share with you some examples:

Anthony Robbins

One of my first mentors, Anthony Robbins, tells of how he was penniless and living in a one room apartment and had to wash his dishes in the bathtub. He has gone on to motivate and change thousands upon thousands of other people's lives, including mine. In the process he has become exceedingly financially successful. (When we serve others, we attract untold riches to ourselves.)

Terrance Stanley Fox

Terry Fox is another person who made a huge impact on other people's lives by using his situation for good rather than focusing on his own problem.

Terry Fox was born in Winnipeg, Manitoba, Canada. After losing his right leg at age 20 to Cancer, this young athlete decided to run from coast to coast in order to raise money for cancer research. Beginning at St. John's, Newfoundland on April 12, 1980, he aimed to finish his run at Vancouver, British Columbia. He ran an average of 42 km a day—the distance of a typical marathon. No one had ever done anything similar to the task he was undertaking.

As the cancer spread to his lung, he was forced to abandon the course on September 1, 1980 just north-east of Thunder Bay, Ontario after 143 days, running 5,373 km (3,339 miles) through Newfoundland, Nova Scotia, Prince Edward Island, New Brunswick, Quebec, and Ontario. A few days later, Canada's CTV network telecasted a telethon to raise money for cancer research and to, in spirit, keep Fox's Marathon of Hope going. Many Canadian and Hollywood celebrities took part in the event which raised more than $10 million.

Despite the setback, Fox wasn't ready to admit defeat, and on several occasions in the fall of 1980 there were reports that the runner might be well enough to resume his marathon. Terry Fox died on June 28, 1981 at the age of 22, one month before his 23rd birthday. Terry Fox run events have raised more than $400M for cancer research. Mt. Terry Fox in British Columbia, near Valemont, is named after him.

Oprah Winfrey

Everyone knows who Oprah Winfrey is.

Oprah's childhood was spent being bounced around from mother to grandmother to Dad to mother, running away from home, to Dad (Vernon Lee) and back to mother. Oprah spent her first six years living in rural poverty with her grandmother, Hattie Mae Lee, who was so poor that Oprah often wore dresses made of potato sacks, for which the local children made fun of her. Her grandmother would hit her with a switch when she did not do chores or if she misbehaved in any way.

Oprah was molested by a cousin when she was nine and her mother, between being poor and having other children, could not cope with Oprah.

Despite these challenges, Oprah drew from her childhood experiences the positive encouragement she received from her grandmother to speak in public and Vernon Lee's strict but encouraging emphasis on education. She has used her success to help others and through her private charity, The Oprah Winfrey Foundation, she has awarded hundreds of grants to organizations that support the education and empowerment of women, children and families in the United States and around the world. She has donated millions of dollars toward providing a better education for students who have merit but no means and she also created "The Oprah Winfrey Scholars Program," which gives scholarships to students determined to use their education to give back to their communities in the United States and abroad.

The Oprah Winfrey Foundation gave gifts of food, clothing, athletic shoes, school supplies, books and toys to more than 50,000 children in orphanages and rural schools in South Africa and provided sixty-three schools with libraries and teacher education.

Oprah established The Oprah Winfrey Leadership Academy Foundation, to which she has contributed more than $40 million toward the creation of the Oprah Winfrey Leadership Academy for Girls—South Africa, which opened in January 2007 and now serves grades 7 through 12. The Leadership Academy is a state-of-the-art independent school that engenders high standards of academic achievement and service leadership for girls from all nine South African provinces who show outstanding promise despite their impoverished backgrounds and social circumstances. Her vision is that the Leadership Academy will help develop the future women leaders of South Africa.

In a 1997 episode of *The Oprah Winfrey Show*, Oprah encouraged viewers to use their lives to make a difference in the lives of others, which led to the creation of the public charity Oprah's Angel Network in 1998. Oprah's Angel Network has raised more than $80 million, with 100 percent of the donations funding charitable projects and grants across the globe.

If you had a terrible childhood, so what? Did it teach you lessons that have helped you to cope with problems and become a better person? So what if your husband left you? What opportunities do you have open to you now? So what if you have financial problems? Perhaps it means things can only get better. I am not by any means minimizing your pain or experience, I am merely pointing out that you can choose to view your challenges differently. Refuse to be a victim; become the victor. Think of challenges as gifts of opportunities to become a better you—however you may define that "better you." Ultimately, what this all boils down to is that you cannot continue to live in the past.

If you live in the past, you won't get to your future. Look at your past only to understand it, but look forward to your future with the positive expectation that when you decide to take charge and act, you can determine your future's outcome. As Kierkegaard, the German philosopher, stated, ***"Life is often understood backwards but must be lived forwards."***

Your New Story

You know what your story is up to this point. You can look back on it to understand that it has brought you to where you are today. Don't get stuck in your past. Don't wonder "What if?" You have no control over the past, and you cannot change it. The only thing you can change is how you think about it. Take from your past the valuable lessons it has taught you, and be resolved to start living your new story. How do you want your life to unfold? What are your dreams? Be clear about them. What do you need to do? What price will you pay? Move your feet and go confidently toward your dreams.

Summary

- Your name, your work does not define you.
- Your race, religion, your gender does not define you.
- You have been programmed from childhood but you can de-program what doesn't serve you.
- It doesn't matter what you have been told, it is your interpretation that makes it real for you.
- It isn't what happens to you, it's what you do with what happens to you.
- You are unique.
- Your true essence is who you are at your inner core, irrespective of anything or anyone else.
- If you live in the past you won't get to your future.
- Use the lessons you have learned from your past to start living your new life.

Chapter 8

This Sums It Up—Accept and Use Your Challenges

Be calm and strong and patient. Meet failure and disappointment with courage. Rise superior to the trials of life and never give in to hopelessness or despair. In danger and adversity, cling to your principles and ideals.

Sir William Osler in "Aequanimitas"

IN LIFE, YOU CAN ALWAYS expect to face challenges, but when we're given challenges, we need to remember that we're never given challenges we do not have the strength to overcome. In fact, the greatest growth comes from your greatest challenge.

See every challenge as an opportunity to be more of who you are.

Alex Martin Neely

A pessimist sees the difficulty in every opportunity.
An optimist sees the opportunity in every difficulty.

Sir Winston Churchill

A pessimist is one who makes difficulties of his opportunities. An optimist is one who makes opportunities of his difficulties.

Harry S. Truman

If Thomas Edison were to have stopped in his efforts to invent the light bulb, we would not have electricity today. In fact, he had thousands of failures in his efforts to invent the light bulb. My everyday advice is, when you're handed lemons make lemonade. We can live our lives going aimlessly nowhere. Choose instead to do something to make your life count. At the end of our lives when we're gone, people whose lives we have touched should feel that they were better off having known us. We all need to find our life purpose. We need to find it and live it. Just like a car cannot move without an engine, we cannot move without our inner power or inner strength. We need to identify our engine, i.e. our inner power or inner strength.

When we are given challenges just know that there are lessons to be learned from them. In the face of challenges, simply analyze the situation and implement the W.H.A.M. method, as discussed earlier, in order to handle your problems or challenges. Ask: What is the problem? How does that make me feel? Ask: Is the situation acceptable or is it changeable? If your situation is one that can be changed, ask what do I need to do in order to change the situation? Lastly, move your feet to effect the change. In order to make the right decisions, you need to know who you are at your inner core. The most important ingredient is taking action, because if you fail to take action nothing changes, and if you want change, you need to take action. You need to know where you are, where you want to go, and what you have to do to get there.

Summary

- In the middle of every challenge is an opportunity.
- Be an optimist, not a pessimist.
- When life hands you lemons, make lemonade.
- Find a purpose and live it.
- Make your life count.
- Use your inner strength to move you toward your goal.
- Handle challenges using the W.H.A.M. method:
    - What's the problem?
    - How do I feel?
    - (Is it) Acceptable or changeable?
    - Move my feet to make changes.
- There are lessons to be learned from every challenge.

Chapter 9

What's Holding You Back?

WE GIVE MANY REASONS WHY we do not take action—lack of time, lack of money, lack of knowledge or education, etc. etc. Fear seems to be the number one thing that holds us back. It holds us back from taking the crucial steps toward accomplishing our dreams.

Had the early settlers not ventured out in search of their dreams, America as we know it would not exist. Many modern day appliances and technology would not have been invented or discovered if someone had not dreamed big enough to take action and pay the price. There are too many people who have never dared to dream or think of anything outside of their everyday, humdrum lives because they fear failure. On the flip side of that is a fear of success. We may believe we do not deserve to be successful or if we are successful we may lose our friends. Have you experienced having many friends in the midst of your suffering but the minute you begin to want to dream, want to succeed, they become fewer in number? Are they really friends if they do not want you to succeed, if they cannot be happy in your success? Sometimes we fail to take that important step toward our dream because we feel it's too big. When you say "I can't" it usually means "I won't." ***You are capable of doing anything your heart desires.***

I was once the little girl who was afraid to speak, and afraid to put my hand up in class because I was so self-conscious. Remember I had been told not to speak unless spoken to and I had deduced that I had nothing important to say. Even if I was sure I knew the answer, by the time I quieted my nerves, by the time I had decided to put my hand up, someone else was invariably called upon to give the answer. On the occasions when I was called to stand up to give the answer, my face went beet red as the blood rushed up to my face, my heart beat went up to ten thousand times a minute, or so it seemed. My knees shook and I stammered. If the answer was correct, I sat down relieved and wondered why I was even afraid in the first place. This was all because of fear and because at that time I did not believe in myself.

Since then I have acquired my Competent Toastmaster Medal and I have been giving workshops, seminars and speeches. Not to mention also, I speak on behalf of others in my current profession. Deep within me I always knew I had a voice and although I was not actively discouraged, I was not encouraged to use it. I first had to believe in myself and I had to believe that I have an important message that others need to hear. My dream is to convey the message to everyone, particularly women, that you do not need to succumb under challenges. Rather accept your challenges as gifts to use as stepping stones to your goal to lead better and more purposeful lives.

What dream lies hidden within you that wants to manifest itself? Have you decided what your big purpose in life is? Have you discovered the real you so that you can live your life congruent with who you are? What do you want to be, do, and have in your life?

The ideal goal is to live all the areas of your life congruent with your true values or inner being. There is what I like to think of as being six different areas in our lives. We have our work—career, job, profession however we earn our living. We have our finances. We have our health. We have our family life. We have relationships with others and we have our spiritual life. There are others, who define them in different ways.

The following speech was delivered by Bryan Dyson, a former CEO of Coca-Cola.

Imagine life is a game in which you're juggling some five balls in air. They are work, family, health, friends and spirit and you're keeping all of these in the air. You will soon understand that work is a rubber ball. If you drop it, it will bounce back, but the other four balls—family, health, friends and spirit—are made of glass. If you drop one of these they will be irrevocably scuffed, marked, nicked, damaged or even shattered. They will never be the same. You must understand and strive for it. You can take from this that you need to work efficiently during office hours and leave on time. Give the required time to your family, friends and have proper rest. Value has a value only if its value is valued.

Rather than believing that one is any more important than the other, I view each area as being a spoke in a wheel and they all have to be functioning at the same level in order for the wheel to turn properly. In other words, you cannot ignore your job and everything else is in top performance and have a functioning life. Likewise, you can't ignore your finances and expect to have a functioning life. Each one works in conjunction with the other.

For instance, if your finances are not in order it affects your relationship. Likewise, it affects your health because you're under pressure worrying about finances. We all know about the mind-body connection, where your thoughts affect your body and that can lead to ulcers and to stress. Worry about finances may even affect your spiritual well-being because you begin to doubt. You begin to wonder if there's some conspiracy and God or your Supreme Being is conspiring against you to make life difficult. When your finances are not in order it can affect your job because you see your work differently. You may see it as only a means to an end, instead of being the outlet that gave you so much satisfaction before. Likewise, if your relationship is not going well you could be directing your energies toward your job as opposed to working on the relationship. They all go hand in hand.

Even though there are times when you need to devote more time to different aspects of your life, you cannot ignore any one of these areas. You need them all to function properly.

Knowing where you're at is so important because you need to establish where you are in order to know which direction to go to reach where you want to be.

Remember the W.H.A.M. method I described earlier.

In my situation, relating to furthering my education, I asked myself, *What is the problem?* The problem was that I had not had the opportunity to go to university and I felt I needed a university degree to progress in my work life. I then asked, *How does that make me feel?* Inadequate, was my answer. Then I asked, *Is that acceptable to me, or do I want to change my situation?* I decided it was not acceptable to me and that I did in fact want to change my situation. Once I had determined how, I *moved* in that direction. You can do whatever you wish, but you have to believe that you can do it. If you think you can or you think you can't, you are right. What will you believe?

Money sometimes holds people back, and that was a big one for me. I didn't view this as a roadblock. Instead I chose to find a solution because my dream was big enough. Dexter Yeager, in his book called *Don't Let Anybody Steal Your Dream,* said, **"If the dream is big enough the problems really don't matter."** Don't focus on the problems, focus on the dreams. Dare to dream. Decide where you want to spend your energy, time and money to reach your goals.

I sold my boss on the idea that my having a university degree was an advantage to the company, making me a more valuable employee. He supported my thinking and convinced the company to subsidize my courses 50 percent once I had received a "C" or better grade. Knowing I needed this subsidy, I applied myself so that my marks guaranteed I only had to pay 50 percent of my tuition fees.

I introduced the concept earlier that if an idea presents itself to you, the way will become clear. This was the first time I had proved to myself that when you have set your goal and you have decided that you are prepared to pay the price (do what has to be done), the information you need will come to you and then you need to take action in order for it to happen. I could have sat back and just wondered how I could ever afford to go to university, and it would never have happened.

I had to work full time because I had a family and I had to take care of my children. There was no support at home, at least not as much as I required. There were sacrifices. Every spare moment I had was used to study—even on the short half-hour commute on the train to work I buried myself deep in my textbook. At lunchtime I ate at my desk while completing my homework. I used my vacation days to write papers or study. When my children were off from school on what we in Canada call PD Days (Professional Development—for the teachers), I took them to Ontario Place, which had a small playground. Yes, it cost a little money, but it allowed them to have playtime and fun while I sat on the grass nearby with my textbook, looking up every so often to check that they were fine. Occasionally they ran up to me to share how much fun they were having. We stopped for a picnic lunch. At the end of the day they were happy, and I was happy because I got my studies done and it wasn't at the expense of my children. The dream consumed me and so I did whatever I needed to do. At my graduation, Mama told me how proud she was of me, and that meant a lot. One of my very best girlfriends, Yvonne, was also there and she told me how proud she was of me. My children said the same. I believe, more importantly, I was proud of me. I had set my sights on a university degree, and never took my sights off my goal; I paid the price and I attained my goal. This experience is one I draw upon time and again whenever I want to achieve something else. So if you have ever achieved a goal in your life, reflect back on how you felt, how you acted in order to achieve the goal, and duplicate your belief, your emotions, and your actions to accomplish your next goal.

My sons Chris and Steve at my graduation from York University.

Countless individuals stop themselves in their tracks by saying, "I don't know how." Accurately assessing your condition is important, and admitting you don't know *how* is a start. But don't stop there. Focus on *what* it is you need to know, ask the questions in your mind, ask them of other people, and the answers will come. What you focus upon appears. I recall that as soon as I purchased my Toyota RAV4, everywhere I went I saw a Toyota RAV4 whereas I had not noticed many before.

Do not allow obstacles, life, or challenges to get in your way. Do not let them hold you back. There are no excuses for not taking action in the direction of your dream. If you're on your way to work and there is an accident or heavy traffic, you're not likely to turn around and go back home. Is your life purpose or goal not more important than going to work? You wouldn't give up trying to get into work, so why should you give up on your dream? Your dream is extremely important to you, because in life we need to find our purpose and live it. If your dream is, for instance, to become a published author, are you going to worry about what other people are going to say? Are you going to constantly believe that it's beyond you, that you can't? Are you going to say I need money, I don't have money or I don't know how to do it? Those are simply little hurdles to overcome. Every obstacle has a way around it—over, under or through. All things are possible, if you only believe.

Life will get in the way and I really love the description that author Willie Jolley gives in his book *A Setback is a Setup for a Comeback*. He said, ***"Sometimes you're the windshield, sometimes you're the bug, but even when you're the bug sometimes you can hit that windshield and bounce off and fly away. You do not have to crash and burn."*** We make choices in life; you can choose to be or not to be, the questions are "What's holding you back?" and "Are your fears bigger than your dreams?"

Summary

- Fear is the number one reason for not pursuing our dreams.
- All things are possible if we only believe.
- When your dreams are big enough, the problems really don't matter.
- There are six key areas of life: work, financial, health, relationship with family, relationship with friends, and spiritual.
- Each area requires your full attention to have your life run smoothly.
- Make your dreams bigger than your fears.
- Use the W.H.A.M. method.

Chapter 10

Dare to Dream

ASK YOURSELF "WHAT DO I want to do?" and acknowledge that you can. If you think you can or you think you can't, you're right. So why not choose to think possible. Keep in mind that you do have to know who it is you were meant to be. Your inner core values will tell you what it is that you need to do to be congruent with those values. Discover and examine your values. Ask yourself questions. For instance ask if you are a person of integrity? If you're not sure, think about situations where you had a choice to tell the truth or lie. Did you choose to tell the truth or do the right thing? Ask if you are a kind or a giving person. Think in what ways you have given of your time, your effort and yourself without compensation. Examine what will make you accomplish goals which are in line with your values. For instance, if you are honest and a person of integrity, you perhaps would not do well in sales if you do not believe in the product that you are selling. Your values define who you are and how you live. This is why you need to live consciously to ensure you are living a life that is congruent with your values, otherwise, the misfit results in stress, and yes, even disease. Dr. Deepak Chopra, the mind-body connect guru, reports that dis-ease causes ill health and disease, and many modern day medical professionals are now beginning to understand this.

In the previous chapter I talked about the reasons we give for not pursuing our dreams. My solution to that is FIDO: Forget It and Drive On. We need to replace our fear with the thoughts of the possible. In other words, if I set myself a goal, I need to believe it is possible to accomplish that goal.

If you think you can do a thing or think you can't do a thing, you're right.

Henry Ford

So why not choose to think that you can, so that you find what you need to do and the route you need to take to get to that goal or dream. Let your values guide you. There are too many people doing jobs or living lives that conflict with every part of their being. Consequently, they are not truly happy and will likely make themselves sick simply by being stressed out as a result of living a lie. I use the simple example of a job, but this applies to all aspects of your life, including relationships. If you are involved with someone whose basic or moral values are not what you approve of, the relationship is not a wholesome one. For instance, it is unhealthy to continue in a relationship with a drug addict or a drunk when this is behavior contrary to your values. It is so important to live an authentic life if you are hoping to achieve a goal in life that is congruent with who you are.

It is important to love yourself and overcome any weaknesses you have. In doing so you will develop your strengths and discover your potential. It will lead you to find inner peace and contentment. As mentioned earlier, your mind is very powerful. So are words. If you think it's impossible for you to succeed or achieve financial goals, then you will not be successful or fiscally sound. But if you think possible and think this is what you want to accomplish, then you will find the way as well as the resources you need to reach that goal. Many people give up. They do not want to take that first step of defining their goal, figuring out how to reach it and then taking action. Too often we see the obstacles before we see the road to reach our goals. If you focus on the obstacles then you will never move toward your goals. You need to dream and make that dream big enough so that you will do whatever you can to find the way to reach that dream.

A lot has to do with how you think. My recommendation is to change your thoughts, your mind and your actions, and you will change your results. There is a formula that is used by T. Harv Eker, author of

Secrets of the Millionaire Mind, called TFAR. Your thoughts (T) lead to your feelings (F), which will lead you to actions (A) which will then lead you to results (R).

Life hands you challenges all the time. Accept that and realize that you can sit back, let those challenges rule you, give in to the messages that you're not good enough and don't deserve it, or instead you can dare to dream, find the way, and take that first step toward your dream. A journey of a thousand miles begins with a single step.

> It is not because things are difficult we do not dare,
> it is because we do not dare that things are difficult.
>
> *Seneca*

Make it easy on yourself—dare to dream.

Summary

- Whatever you do, it must be congruent with your inner values.
- Dare to dream big, believe you can accomplish your goal, find the way to reach your goal, then take that first step toward your goal.

Chapter 11

Take Action

O BVIOUSLY, THE FIRST STEP IS to define your goal. You will also need to determine what actions will be necessary to accomplish that goal. However, if we never take that first step, if we never take action, then we will never reach our goal. Sometimes we think of the reasons why we cannot reach our goals, so we take no action.

Be advised, however, *you will need to make a choice*. Life is all about making choices, whether or not you do so consciously. Indeed, by not making a choice, you have in fact chosen. Make the choice to save yourself so you can leave a positive legacy for those that follow you. The right choices can pave the path to a bright and happy future. Choose consciously now to take charge of your life.

We need to make each dream very big and audacious—one that we really want. In other words, this goal is one that we must have and must accomplish, no matter what. If your goal is not important, you won't be prepared to make sacrifices, nor will you put the necessary effort into it and if we do none of those things, then we'll never reach our goal.

As mentioned previously, you need to stay true to who you are, because if your goals are not true to who you are, it's not something your inner being can support so you will not put the effort behind it.

The size of your success is measured by the strength of your desire. The size of your dream and how you handle disappointment along the way.

Robert Kiyosaki

I cannot emphasize enough that your goal must be one that is in congruence with your inner self. In life we each need to find a purpose. The purpose of life is a life of purpose. So once we have defined the goal, we've decided it is truly something we want and that it is in congruence with who we are and what our values are, we need to let that dream consume us. It must be our focus. We need to maintain laser focus and head toward that dream.

Sometimes our dreams can seem huge, almost impossible to reach. The only way to deal with that is to take one step at a time or break it into bite size pieces. When you pursue your dreams, you need to pursue it in confidence, knowing that you are going to achieve it.

> Confidence is going after Moby Dick in a rowboat with tartar sauce.
>
> *Zig Ziglar*

That's confidence!

When you have taken action toward your goal, you need to continue to go toward that goal no matter what challenges present themselves. In other words, you should never quit!

Don't Quit

When things go wrong as they sometimes will,
When the road you're trudging seems all uphill,
When the funds are low and the debts are high,
And you want to smile but you have to sigh,
When care is pressing you down a bit, rest if you must
But don't you quit!

Life is clear with its twists and turns,
As every one of us sometimes learns,
And many a failure turns about,
When he might have won had he stuck it out,
Don't give up, though the pace seems slow,
You may succeed with another blow,

Success is failure turned inside out,
The silver tint of the clouds of doubt,
And you can never tell how close you are,
It may be near when it seems so far,
So stick to the flight, when your heart is hit,
It's when things seem worst that you must not quit!

Author unknown

Here is a story about the importance of not giving up. There was once a bunch of tiny frogs who arranged a climbing competition. The goal was to reach the top of a very high tower. A big crowd had gathered around the tower to see the race and cheer on the contestants. The race began. Honestly, no one in the crowd really believed that the tiny frogs would reach the top of the tower. You heard statements such as "Oh, way too difficult, they will never make it to the top." Or, "Not a chance they will succeed, the tower is too high."

The tiny frogs began collapsing one by one, except for those who, in a fresh burst of energy were climbing higher and higher. The crowd continued to yell, "It is too difficult, no one will make it." More tiny frogs got tired and gave up, but one continued higher and higher. This one wouldn't give up. At the end, everyone else had given up climbing the tower except for the one tiny frog, who after a big effort was the only one who reached the top. Then all the other tiny frogs naturally wanted to know how this one frog managed to do it.

A contestant asked the tiny frog how the strength to reach the goal had been found. The answer was that the winner was deaf.

The wisdom of the story is never to listen to other people's tendencies to be negative or pessimistic, because they take your most wonderful dreams and wishes away from you—the ones you have in your heart. Always think of the power that words have, because everything you hear and read will affect your actions; therefore, always be positive. Above all, be deaf when people tell you that you cannot fulfill your dreams; always think, *I can do this.*

Therefore, in taking action, make sure of the following: (1) you've defined your goal; (2) you've decided how much you want it; (3) you've ascertained that it is in congruence with your inner core; (4) you've let your dream consume you; (5) you've broken the steps down into bite size pieces and (6) taken one step at a time; and (7) you've proceeded with confidence toward your goal while being deaf to detractors and you have not quit. When you follow this formula, there is no doubt that no matter what other challenges life throws at you, success is inevitable.

It is my sincerest wish that you will look past all your struggles, challenges, and conditioning from prior years and that you will dare to dream, take action, move toward your worthwhile dream, and live the life you want and deserve.

Summary

- Nothing happens without action.
- Define your goal.
- Your goal must be one you truly desire.
- Your dream must be in congruence with your inner core.
- Let your dream consume you.
- Break the steps down into bite-size pieces.
- Take one step at a time.
- Move toward your goal in confidence.
- Be deaf to detractors.
- *Never quit!*
- *SUCCEED.*

Chapter 12

Parting Thoughts

I HAVE PROBABLY CONFUSED YOU WITH the amount of information I have shared and with the repetition of what I deem to be so important. Perhaps you find it overwhelming. It doesn't have to be so, and it will make more sense if you digest the information in bite-size pieces.

Also, sometimes we need to receive the information in other media, such as audio or audio-video. This book will be available in CD and MP3 format, which will allow you to re-listen whenever you wish. I invite you to go to my website, http://www.rosepellar-authorspeakertrainer.com, to order the audio version and to receive your access information on my upcoming tele-seminars and workshops and to receive my free newsletter.

In parting, I leave you with an extract that I received by e-mail while I was in the middle of writing this book. It was so appropriate that I just had to share it with you.

In ancient times, a King had a boulder placed on a roadway. Then he hid himself and watched to see if anyone would remove the huge rock. Some of the King's wealthiest merchants and couriers came by and simply walked around it. Many loudly blamed the King for not keeping the roads clear, but none did anything about getting the stone out of the way. Then a peasant came along carrying a load of vegetables. Upon approaching the boulder, the peasant laid down his burden and tried to move the stone to the side of the road. After much pushing and straining, he finally succeeded. After the peasant picked up his load of vegetables, he noticed a purse lying in the road where the boulder had been. The purse contained many gold coins and a note from the King indicating that the gold was for the person who removed the boulder from the roadway. The peasant learned what many of us never understand. **Every obstacle presents an opportunity to improve our condition.**

This message is just what I have been trying to impart throughout this book. If you learn just this one lesson, your life will change.

Namaste.

About the Author

Rose Pellar is a family law attorney practicing in a small town of approximately eighteen thousand people in Ontario, Canada. She is a regular writer for *Women with Vision* magazine.

Rose's life has been anything but easy. However she openly admits that many of the "mistakes" and challenges in her life have proved to be the best things that could have happened to her. She has learned that forgiveness is perhaps the best gift she has given herself, and she is passionate about inspiring women to look past their challenges and to take steps to pursue their goals. She does this through her presentations to women's groups and through seminars and workshops. Rose is living her life making a positive difference in the lives of others.

Rose is happily married and recommits to her marriage daily.